SHE DYED ABOUT

A ROMANTIC CORNER OF THE GARDEN OF LANDOR HOUSE IN EARLY VICTORIAN TIMES. Walter Savage Landor and other members of his family frequented the octagonal summer-house set amongst the tall elms and shrubbery. In the upper corner nearest Chapel Street, there was a square, paved area which was perhaps a secluded, speciality garden. Today this site is a car-park for the occupants of Mitchell House in The Butts—the romance and natural beauty of the garden being long gone. (W.C.R.O.)

(A section of an 1851 map of Warwick)

SHE DYED ABOUT MIDNIGHT

JEAN FIELD

THE STORY OF LANDOR HOUSE,
EASTGATE AND THE COTTAGES IN
SMITH STREET, WARWICK.

BREWIN BOOKS

First published
by Brewin Books, Studley, Warwickshire, B80 7LG
in August 1992

"She Dyed about Midnight"—
see page 44 describing the death of Ann Johnson in 1733.

Cover Photograph shows East Gate and
Landor House in the 1920s

ISBN 1 85858 000 5

**The publication of this book has been facilitated by a grant
from the Trustees of King Henry VIII Charity, Warwick.**

Typeset by Avon Dataset, Bidford on Avon, Warwickshire, B50 4JH
and made and printed by The Cromwell Press, Broughton Gifford, Melksham, Wiltshire.

Contents

TO M.E. LANG

ACKNOWLEDGEMENTS

Much of my research was conducted in Warwickshire County Record Office. I would like to thank the County Archivist and all the staff of the Record Office, in particular Jerry Weber the Senior Conservator who took many of the photographs appearing in this book.

Invaluable help and advice has been given by Miss J. Greenwood, who taught at the King's High School For Girls for many years, latterly as Second Mistress. Her knowledge of the school site is extensive and frequently remarkable. I would like to thank Miss Greenwood and the late Miss D. Whittlesey (previously Second Mistress at K.H.S.W.) for the loan of numerous original photographs.

I am grateful to Mrs P. Molnar for allowing me to use letters which were written to her by Eleanor Doorly.

I would also like to thank Mr J.R. Adcock (Owner of Eastgate) Mrs J.M. Anderson (Headmistress of K.H.S.W.) Mr P. Butler (Clerk to the Trustees of The Charity of King Henry VIII) Mr J.E. Francis (Chairman of Governors of K.H.S.W.) Major M.A. Gaffney (Town Clerk of Warwick) Mr C.E.R. Houghton (Clerk to the Trustees of The United Charities of Richard Griffin and Others) Rev. W.R. Large (Vicar of St Chad's, Bishops Tachbrook) Peters Library Service Ltd (Sponsors of the Carnegie Medal) and Mr S. Miles (Caretaker of K.H.S.W.) besides numerous other people who have related their reminiscences or helped in other ways.

The photographs appearing on pages 10, 16, 40, 55, 64, 68, 70, 72, 82, 83, 88 (top), 91, 97, 102, 106, 112, 113, 120, 125 and 162 are reproduced by courtesy of Warwickshire County Record Office and that on page 93 by courtesy of Birmingham Reference Library.

BIBLIOGRAPHY

VICTORIA COUNTY HISTORY OF WARWICKSHIRE — Volumes 2 and 8
A HISTORY OF WARWICK AND ITS PEOPLE — T. Kemp 1905
WARWICK CHARITIES 1826 — H.M. Commissioners
THE TOWN MAPS OF WARWICK 1610-1851 — W.C.R.O.
WORTHIES OF WARWICKSHIRE — F.L. Colvile 1869
COMPLETE PEERAGE — Edited Gibbs. 1910
WARWICKSHIRE IN 1790 — P. Lavery 1974
HISTORY OF WARWICKSHIRE — Will. Smith 1830
THE RESTORATION OF THE BEAUCHAMP CHAPEL — Ed. Dugdale 1956
WALTER SAVAGE LANDOR — Forster 1869
WALTER SAVAGE LANDOR — M. Elwin 1941 (Also Replevin 1958)
WALTER SAVAGE LANDOR — R. Super 1957
THE LETTERS OF W.S. LANDOR — Ed. S. Wheeler 1899
ROBERT EYRES LANDOR — Eric Partridge 1927
BAZAAR AND MAYDAY FESTIVAL 1895 — Notes by T.E. Brigden
SAMUEL PARR'S MEMOIRS 1828
THE OFFCHURCH STORY — K. Swanzy 1968
DR WILLIAM LAMBE—H. Saxe Wydham 1940 (London Vegetarian Soc.)
THE HISTORY OF WARWICK SCHOOL — A. Leach 1906
THE BOOK OF THE JUBILEE (K.H.S.W.) 1929
CHRONICLE OF THE TWENTIETH CENTURY—Longmans 1988
THE KING'S HIGH SCHOOL 1879-1979 (The Governors)
WHO'S WHO IN WARWICKSHIRE IN 1934 — E. Baylis
WARWICK ITS PRESERVATION AND DEVELOPMENT — Nickson and
Abercrombie — Architectural Press 1949
IN THE REALMS OF GOLD (Carnegie Medal) — K. Barker 1986
THE DEVELOPMENT OF EDUCATION IN WARWICKSHIRE IN THE
NINETEENTH CENTURY — James 1971 (Xerox of typescript in W.C.R.O.)
Various editions of 'Warwick and Warwickshire Advertiser'
Kelly's, Spennell's, White's, Pigot's, West's, & P.O. Directories of Warwickshire

INTRODUCTION

Over forty years ago, like thousands of other pupils before me, I was lucky enough to attend a school which used as part of its premises a group of old buildings at the top of Smith Street in Warwick; namely the old Eastgate of the town, two tudor cottages and a fine town house, built in the reign of William and Mary, known as Landor House.

Soon after leaving school, as part of a college project, I wrote an investigation into the history of the buildings. The more I discovered, the more my interest grew.

The late Mr E. G. Tibbits assisted me enormously with my research. Whilst researching the subject in 1957, I was referred to Mr Tibbits who was then Clerk to the Trustees of the United Charities of Richard Griffin and others. In 1956 a chest containing documents relating to the Ann Johnson Charity Trust had been discovered in a vault under the Court House and Mr Tibbits, a local solicitor and historian, was attempting to sort and catalogue the material.

Recently whilst reading some of the documents, now housed in the Warwick County Record Office, I have been reminded of the precise, forthright and enthusiastic Mr Tibbits, as labels bearing his handwriting were affixed to several bundles. I had been led to believe that Mr Tibbits would write a book on the subject, but when I had time to return to my investigations over thirty years later, I found that no book had ever been written.

Many early documents relating to Landor House and the cottages are still in existence today because after the death of the original owners of Landor House, Dr William Johnson and his wife Ann, a charity trust was set up whereby the property was let and the income used to help the poor and needy. James Fish the Younger, a surveyor who had assisted the Johnsons in the management of their affairs, became the Chief Trustee of the Charity and not only did he help preserve the many documents amassed by the family, but he wrote numerous lists and accounts in his own neat handwriting.

For me, reading the memoranda of the meticulous James Fish was the most enjoyable part of the research. He often made odd jottings on odd scraps of paper and to follow his asterisks and pointing fingers, was to share a secret undisclosed for over 250 years! I like to think that it was the efficient Mr Fish who caused the numerous papers to be stored in the chest in the first place. So far as is possible, I have used original material when compiling this book, but naturally, with a time-span of over 500 years, many books were used as background material. When describing more recent times, I have included the reminiscences of various local people, as I feel that such first-hand accounts are invaluable when trying to create a true picture of the past.

As the history of buildings tends to be rather dull, I have concentrated on the many wonderful characters who have been connected with the premises, either as inhabitants or frequent visitors. Dog-lovers, unruly children and broken-hearted parents—all are represented here.

Why was Henry Johnson left only a few shillings by his wealthy parents? Why did Walter Savage Landor squander a large fortune and refuse to go hunting? Which Doctor ate raw potato for breakfast? The story is a fascinating one!

EARLY HISTORY
EASTGATE AND THE ORIGINAL
COTTAGES PRE 1690

Our story starts with Ethelfleda, the Lady of the Mercians!

In 914 A.D. Ethelfleda, the daughter of King Alfred the Great, fortified the town of Warwick, along with nine other small towns, in an effort to protect the borders of the Kingdom of Mercia against the invading Danes.

Ethelfleda recognised the potential of the town, situated on a hill and easily defendable. There was plenty of good building stone and well water, so the town was suited for development.

Accordingly, on Ethelfleda's instructions, a ditch was dug around Warwick and a simple earthen wall constructed.

After the Norman Conquest, the Castle was begun in 1068 and the first mention of town gates seems to have been around this time. It seems likely that Turchil of Arden, the Saxon Earl then owner of Warwick, constructed a ditch round the town and gated it, on the orders of William the Conqueror. The ditch probably followed the line of that planned by Ethelfleda over a century and a half previously.

Eastgate, the Town Walls and Punishments.

Not only did the Plantagenet King Edward I erect the beautiful memorial crosses wherever the body of his first wife Eleanor rested, as it was brought from Nottingham to London, he also enacted many statutes, which made for reforms in government. One statute commanded that all great towns were to be walled, with the gates closed from sunset till sunrise and watchmen on the alert during the night. Being an important town, Warwick would have had to comply with this statute; in fact the Borough Seal, little changed since 1545 when first introduced, seems to show the town walls at night during this period, with watchmen blowing horns.

At some period during the thirteenth century, the previous earth rampart was partly rebuilt in stone, probably the sections near the town gates. Even today, a sizeable section of the town wall remains to the north of Westgate and a small section on the north side of Eastgate.

As the Castle defended the approach to the south, there were three main gates; the Eastgate, Westgate and Northgate. By the early sixteenth century, this Northgate had been demolished and the East and West gates substantially reconstructed. Today the East and West gates are different in size and style, the length of the

*THE BATTLEMENTS OF EAST-
GATE provide a wonderful vantage
point. The battlements on the south side
are shown here, with the former Castle
Arms to the right.*

*THE REMAINS OF THE TOWN
WALL AND THE STONE STEPS
LEADING TO ST PETER'S CHA-
PEL. Although the steps have been
reconstructed and resurfaced, this is probably the oldest part of the entire site. The
Town Wall probably dates from the
fourteenth century and on pre 1788
illustrations can be clearly seen. These
same steps would have been used by
thousands of charity school pupils over
the centuries as they made their way into
the Bablake School held in St Peter's
Chapel and they are still in occasional use
today.*

VIEW FROM THE BATTLEMENTS OF EASTGATE.

The view down Smith Street, towards Leamington and the East.

passage of Eastgate being 46 feet, but that of the barrel vaulted passage of Westgate, nearly double that length.

The Eastgate, as it is today, probably dates from the fourteenth century, but having been reconstructed in the early fifteenth century, when a chapel was built above. Certainly, the passage of Eastgate remains a place to fire the imagination! It is easy to conjure up a scene typical of five hundred years ago, with rough carts, peasants and wealthy horse riders passing through the gateway.

In Medieval times, the gateways of towns were the obvious places to site warnings and the gates of Warwick were often used for this purpose. How many severed heads or quartered remains of supposed wrongdoers were exhibited on the East, North and West gates, we can only surmise.

There are some accurate records of such happenings as in 1604, when an elderly Roman Catholic priest was condemned to be hanged, drawn and quartered, after being held for a year in Warwick Prison. The quartered remains of the 70 year old John Sugar must have been a ghastly sight, set up on the East and West gates, to deter others from adopting a similar religious faith. A few months previously, there had been cases of the plague in Warwick and it was in hottish weather, 16th July 1604, that poor Sugar's remains were set up. Warwick in those days was no place for the squeamish—afraid of dirt, flies, rats or disease!

The view to the West, showing Jury Street and Westgate barely visible beyond the houses.

A few years previously, another Roman Catholic priest William Freeman, otherwise Mason, had suffered a similar fate on 13th August 1595.

Before St Peter's Chapel was built above the gateway, the battlements and the walkway along the town walls would have been particularly important. Even today, there is a fine view of the approaches from the battlements of Eastgate.

Perhaps the practice has been discontinued, but some years ago, it was the custom to take all new pupils of the King's High School on a guided tour of the battlements in order to enliven lessons on Medieval architecture. The pupils found the experience fascinating, but the inhabitants of Warwick were often rather alarmed to see 30 girls peering down at them!

The Town Ditch.

When the walls were partly rebuilt in stone during the Middle Ages, the ditch was retained and possibly made much larger. At one stage, the ditch appears to have been 25 feet wide and 9 feet deep in places.

Eventually the ditch was filled in, probably not systematically, but haphazardly, whenever rubble or rubbish needed to be buried.

It seems that the Town Wall and Ditch extended from Eastgate across ground which now forms part of the gardens of houses in The Butts which back onto Chapel Street. Interestingly in 1965, when building work near the Playground Entrance to the King's High School For Girls was begun, firm foundations became difficult when it was discovered that the site was 'made up ground'. Eventually a pile driver was used to penetrate 30 feet down, but without extensive excavation of the area, it is impossible to say for certain that the site was indeed that of the former Town Ditch.

St Peter's Chapel Is Built.

Sometime during the reign of Henry VI, probably around 1426, a chapel dedicated to St Peter was built above the Eastgate. An earlier St Peter's Church had stood in High Street, near the junction with Castle Street, but by the end of the fourteenth century, this church was in ruins.

The new chapel was maintained and a chantry priest supplied by the Guild of Warwick, which was an amalgamation of the two old Guilds of St George the Martyr and Holy Trinity & St Mary. The Guilds had been formed in 1383, but between 1392 and 1415, they amalgamated.

The Guild of Warwick supplied four priests to sing masses, the three others being concerned with St James' Chapel over Westgate and the Chapel of Our Lady (completed in 1462 and better known as the Beauchamp Chapel) in St Mary's church.

Access to St Peter's Chapel was via stone steps to the left of the Pedestrian Arch inside the town walls. Although much restored, these same steps are still used occasionally.

For over a hundred years, it seemed that the Guild Chapel flourished. Pilgrims visited it, but at no stage does it appear to have attracted wealthy support.

In 1535, John Wattwood was the priest, for which he was paid £13 6 8d annually. The famous historian Leyland visited Warwick in 1538 and he wrote,

"There is over the East gate a goodly Chappell of St Peter..... The suburbe without the East Gate is called Smithes Street (The Jews sometimes dwelled in it)"

In 1545 numerous changes to the government of Warwick came about. The Guild sold land to establish a kind of trust, which was to provide the town with funds to run St Mary's Church and the King's Grammar School, besides cover other necessary expenditure. The Guild was then dissolved and power transferred to the new corporation.

So the main income of the town came from King Henry VIII's Estate, as the fund came to be known. The two Wardens of the Guild before its dissolution, Thomas Oken and Thomas Roo, played a large part in the activities of the new corporation; so in effect a smooth changeover of power occurred, to the subsequent benefit of the town.

St Peter's Chapel Is In Ruins.

After the Guild of Warwick was dissolved, both Guild Chapels over the gates of the town fell into disrepair. St Peter's over Eastgate and St James' over Westgate

THE OUTSIDE ENTRANCE TO ST PETER'S CHAPEL was the only means of entry until 1918, when an inside staircase was built. Thousands of Charity School pupils must have used this entrance to The Bablake School.

were barely used at all and the town obviously had a problem as to what to do with the buildings. By 1571, St Peter's was "Ruinous and ready to fall" according to John Fisher, the Town Clerk, in a letter to London.

Eventually a deal was struck which ended with money for repairs being found. The Earl of Leycester (brother to the Earl of Warwick) wanted the old Guildhall, St James' Chapel and other buildings near Westgate, in order to found his hospital. In 1571, the town granted the Earl the buildings and in return, it was to receive the Shire Hall and money to repair St Peter's.

It was not until 1576 that the Earls of Warwick and Leycester performed their side of the bargain. In that year an agreement granted to the Bailiff and Burgesses of Warwick,

"All that building or Chapel above a gate called the East Gate (vocatum le Eastgate) with a piece of waste land between the chapel and the wall a tenement in the occupation of Margaret Haley widow."

The general idea was that the King's Grammar School, which had been in difficulties over premises since the loss of the Guild Banqueting Hall to the Earl of Leycester, should use St Peter's when repaired. Repairs were carried out, but it is not known whether the King's School ever did use the chapel—probably not. Eventually, the King's School moved into other premises, first in the Market Square and after the Great Fire, into a building in The Butts.

St Peter's Chapel remained Corporation property till 1590, when it was taken into Crown hands on the death of Ambrose Dudley, Earl of Warwick, along with other buildings. However in 1595, the Crown leased the property to the town corporation for 40 years.

As the corporation seemed to have little use for St Peter's Chapel, it was leased to local landowners, who probably sub-let the building for use as a dwelling.

In 1600, St Peter's was granted to Richard Dawes and Thomas Wagstaffe (an important local landowner) but in the same year, they sold it to William Spicer, who also owned the cottages adjoining Eastgate. William Spicer sold the property back to the corporation, who continued to lease it to local men.

On 21st Nov. 1615, an entry in the Corporation Minute Book agreed,

"That William Carter be put in possession of St Peter's Chappell and that the same be let to Richard Goodwick at will from yeare to yeare at 20 shillings a yeare and keeping repaire."

Again in the Minute Book, there is an entry dated 20th February 1677, which showed that the chapel was let to Richard Bromley for 27 years at a rent of £1 17 6d per annum.

There were numerous members of the Bromley family living in Warwick in the seventeenth century and Richard and his wife had a number of children. Son John was born in 1684 and daughter Mary in 1690. Twins Thomas and Susan were born in St Peter's in 1693, just at the time when Landor House was being reconstructed from an earlier dwelling and the area around Eastgate must have been bustling with activity at that time.

Presumably Richard Bromley remained the tenant until 1700 when St Peter's Chapel was converted into a schoolroom. Apart from a few decades, a schoolroom it has remained ever since!

The Property Between Eastgate and Chapel Street.

Originally four dwellings occupied the area of Smith Street between the town wall and Chapel Street. The two cottages nearest Eastgate still remain and it is thought

IS THIS JANE TORVILE?
The deed signed in 1656 (transferring ownership of the remaining cottages) is interesting as a sketch of a woman and a dog appears inside the initial letter. As did Mr E. G. Tibbits, I like to think that this is a drawing of Jane Torvile and her pet mastiff! (W.C.R.O.)

that they were built around 1500, the first adjacent to or over the site of the former town ditch. The two middle cottages were smaller then the other two and the four dwellings were split into two pairs, to form two houses. The house on the corner of Chapel Street appears to have been bigger, with a large first floor room, similar to a medieval solar or living room. This house also had a wing (probably incorporating two or more former dwellings) housing kitchens and domestic rooms, alongside Chapel Street. In 1693 this larger house was partially demolished and reconstructed to form the present Landor House.

The Remaining Cottages.

The earliest deeds show that for much of the first half of the seventeenth century, these houses were in the hands of a family named Spicer. However as it was the custom for a family name to be passed on to the next generation (as it is still in parts of the U.S.A. and elsewhere) it was sometimes rather difficult to work out exactly who had been concerned in a transaction.

The following is a summary of transactions concerning these cottages.

1596   George Weal (of St Clements, Co. Middlesex, yeoman) sold them to William Spicer the younger.

1603   William Spicer sold them to Thomas Wagstaffe for £100.

1608/9 William Spicer bought back the cottages from the Wagstaffe family.

1629   William Spicer's widow Phillippa made them over to her son, yet another William Spicer!

1638   William Spicer bought some ground at the back of the cottages.

1642   The Spicer family sold them to Jane Torvile (of Trevallyn, Co. Denbigh, a widow)

1656   Jane Torvile sold them to Robert Heath (gentleman) together with the orchard and garden, for £130. At that time, the cottages were let to John Woodward, Gentleman, and Dorothy, his wife.

1670   Some time previous to this date, the cottages were let to a family named Moody, for in the Hearth Tax Returns of 1670, Moody, presumably a baker, had five hearths, one of them being an oven, for which exemption was claimed.

It would appear that the Spicer family were important in Warwick during the later sixteenth and first half of the seventeenth century.

William Spicer, presumably the purchaser in 1596, was Town Clerk (following the famous John Fisher who compiled "The Black Book of Warwick" and "The Book of John Fisher") from 1590 to his death in 1611. Three times William Spicer, along with another burgess John Townsend, was M.P. for Warwick and on his death he was buried in the nearby St Nicholas' Church. It is not known whether the Spicer family actually lived in the cottages or merely invested in the property and leased it out. Circumstances would appear to indicate that the family actually lived in the pleasantly situated property, with the extensive grounds to the rear.

The Houses Partly Demolished When Landor House Was Built.

Far fewer deeds exist for these houses. The earliest shows that in 1641 Richard Bolt (a gentleman of Surrey) bought them from Robert Harvey. In 1652 Richard Bolt sold them to George Weal (the son or grandson of the vendor of the remaining cottages in 1596?)

The Weal family lived in the property for many years and were obviously important citizens of Warwick. From 1664–5, George Weal served as Mayor of Warwick and in 1670, the Hearth Tax Return showed that he was paying tax on six hearths, thus indicating his wealth.

Around 1686, the Weal family moved and let the property (later mortgaging it) to William Tarver, another prominent member of the town Corporation. From 1690 onwards, the ownership of the houses caused many arguments, which ended with a costly lawsuit when Dr William Johnson attempted to buy with a view to extensive reconstruction.

From around 1687, like so many other towns in England, Warwick became divided over circumstances leading to the 'Bloodless Revolution' of 1689, when James II was deposed. Those concerned with the property, George Weal (and after his death his family) William Tarver and Dr William Johnson were all to be involved in a bitter political row in Warwick which caused much controversy. It may well have been that the arguments over the ownership of the property were fuelled by the rows in local politics, especially during 1689.

DR WILLIAM JOHNSON AND HIS FAMILY.

Around 1675, Dr William Johnson arrived in Warwick, which was at that time a thriving place. The population of the town was increasing and there were good opportunities for professional men. Within twenty years, Dr Johnson was to purchase all four cottages and have a fine new town house built in place of two of them.

A Physician.

Well qualified physicians were rare in those times and some towns had only an apothecary to mix and sell drugs. Dr Johnson already possessed considerable medical knowledge when he arrived and in 1683, he was granted a licence from The Royal College of Physicians in London.

The licence granted to Dr Johnson in 1683 is now in Warwick County Record Office. Considering its age, the licence is in surprisingly good condition, with the large seal (protected by a small tin box) still attached to its faded red and blue plaited ribbons.

Probably the only properly qualified physician in Warwick at that time, Dr Johnson must have had an extremely lucrative career. He was called upon to attend many of the rich and titled families living in the area, so the money rolled in!

We know that in 1688, Dr Johnson attended Sir John Knightley of Offchurch Bury in his last illness and in 1697, the Doctor was paid £1 for a visit to Offchurch to attend Sir John's heir, a young man named John Wightwick.

Generally, Dr Johnson used an old style coach known as a chariot to travel to his patients. Popular in the late seventeenth century, in his diary Samuel Pepys mentioned buying a similar vehicle.

Born in 1643, Dr Johnson (often spelt Johnston) had spent much of his early life in Northern Ireland, where his father owned estates in County Down, between Lisburn and Belfast. When William came to England, the rest of the family continued to live in Ireland, although some cousins were living in Liverpool, which was then the crossing port for Ireland.

Like most people at that time, Dr William and his wife Ann were devout churchgoers and there are many records of their children in St Mary's Parish Register. Altogether the Johnsons had eight children; Edward born in 1677, Henry in 1678, Digby in 1680, Ursula in 1681, Ann in 1683, Diana in 1686, Katherine in 1687 and James in 1688.

The fact that the Johnson's last child was named James may have been significant as Dr William seemed to have sympathy for the cause of the Roman Catholic King James II.

1688 Much Bitterness in Warwick.

In 1685 the highly unpopular James had followed his brother King Charles II to the throne, amid mounting tension. As in Ireland today, religion was connected to the general struggle for power. King Charles II had been sensible in many ways and whilst secretly sympathising, had not openly favoured Roman Catholics. James II however was arrogant and from the start openly tried to control Parliament and the Town Corporations, furthering the Roman Catholic cause wherever possible.

Warwick had a long history of being 'Anti-Papist' and from 1687 onwards, there were many arguments concerning William Eades, the newly appointed young Vicar of St Mary's Church, whom the Corporation accused of having pro Catholic leanings.

In 1687 George Weal, then owner of the Smith Street property, had been created an Alderman to give support to the Vicar. However, the Corporation fearing the King was about to interfere, voted to place the revenues from the King Henry VIII Estate (the source of most Corporation money) in the hands of Trustees, as a precaution. King James did interfere and in the summer of 1688, the Corporation was suspended and a Royal Warrant issued in September proposed a new Corporation, consisting almost entirely of Roman Catholics.

A month before James Johnson had been born, King James' wife had borne him a son and heir, Prince James Francis Edward (The Old Pretender) and most people in Warwick hated the idea. In November 1688, poor James Johnson died at the age of only three months and King James II also fared badly. He was forced to flee the country, allowing the Protestant William and Mary jointly to take over the Sovereignty of Britain.

National affairs might have been settled by this 'Bloodless Revolution' but in Warwick the bitterness continued. The old Corporation resumed office and the attacks on Rev. Eades began again. In 1689, the Corporation led by William Tarver accused Rev. Eades of attending the consecration of a Roman Catholic Chapel some time previously.

Having been Mayor from 1684–5, William Tarver had again been asked to take office. When the allegations were made, Dr Johnson incurred the wrath of many by giving the Vicar an alibi—saying that he was with him at his house, for the entire duration of the stone laying ceremony at the R.C. Chapel. James Fish, the Parish Clerk of St Mary's, and his son were also implicated for allegedly ringing the bells and in April 1690, two ex-mayors of the town were ordered to attend a hearing in London.

In the end a compromise was reached and the Vicar remained until 1706, but with a limited income, the Mastership of the King's Grammar School being taken from him. However from 1690 onwards Dr Johnson had various problems, which involved him in several law suits and it may have been that certain Warwick residents were unable to forgive him for siding with the unpopular young Vicar.

The Law Suit With William Tarver.

With seven children ranging in ages from three to thirteen years, the 47 year old Dr Johnson and his wife Ann aged 41, decided they needed a larger house, so in 1690, an attempt was made by Dr Johnson to buy the property on the corner of Chapel Street. The house was owned by Eleanor Weal, the widow of George and negotiations were hampered by the fact that William Tarver was leasing the property and he and his family were reluctant to move. A few years previously William Tarver had taken out a mortgage on the property, which he wished to purchase.

In Warwick County Record Office is a fascinating bundle of letters written at various times by William Tarver to Dr Johnson. Being a cautious and methodical couple, the Johnsons seemed to keep much of their correspondence.

Some of the letters relate to the unpleasantness of the Chancery Suit against Rev. Eades and in general the tone of the letters was polite, even friendly. On 31st December 1691, William Tarver wrote to Dr Johnson,

"My wife and I return you and Madam Johnston our most hearty thanks for your kinde and noble present. But for my part I must also blame you & Mr Edes for treateing your Chancery man soo much. For it is the way to prolong your cause. But in hopes you will now take warning; I will do my best to get you a speedy deliverance."

William Tarver seemed an educated and fair-minded man but negotiations to buy the house dragged on for several years and were only ended when a Chancery Decree was obtained by Dr Johnson early in 1693.

The lawsuit cost Dr Johnson a great deal of money, well over £500 and one wonders why the sale of the property was that important to him. It may have been that William Weal, who was advising his mother Eleanor, was the real cause of the trouble, being determined to sell to the highest bidder. It could have been that various prominent citizens of Warwick conspired together in an effort to thwart Dr Johnson and his plans, because he sided with Rev. Eades against the Corporation.

Ann Johnson's Letter.

Like most innocent parties in a dispute, Ann Johnson became thoroughly disgruntled about the whole affair. Amongst the documents relating to the Johnsons, there is what appeared to be the rough draft of a letter Ann Johnson had written to the wife of Sir John Mordaunt, of Walton Hall, Wellesbourne Hastings, who had been asked to adjudicate in the affair.

THE DESIGNS FOR LANDOR HOUSE.
*Roger Hurlbut submitted two designs for the front elevation of the house. The plainer design on
the left was chosen by Dr Johnson and comparison with a photograph of the house in modern
times indicates how little the present exterior differs from the drawing. (W.C.R.O.)*

In the letter Ann had written,
"Madam, I had not the confidenc to wright to Sr John, but the many
testimonys of your freindship incuraged me to give you this troble.
I fear some malicious bodie or other has bin prejudising Sr John against
us... it is soe great an afliction to me I can not expres, I being and my
children lick to be the greatest sufferers... I need not say anything as to the
justic of the caus to soe deserning a person as your self, you are aquainted
enough in that mater, or you could not have soe wisely descorced with will
weal, to pump out the knavery of the buisnes."
Poor Ann ended, "I beg you good Madam to put Sr John in mind of
what I wright and if you pleas let him se my poor scrible wich I hope both
he and you will pardon."

One could not fail to be moved by such a letter. Undated, it was full of crossings out

LITTLE CHANGED SINCE ITS ERECTION IN 1692/3, THE EXTERIOR OF LANDOR HOUSE IS PARTICULARLY ATTRACTIVE. The style of the windows annoys some architectural purists, but the doorway, with its painted stone surround, is generally admired.

and merely signed A.J. but the handwriting would appear to be that of Ann Johnson.

The Agreement With Roger Hurlbut. September 1st 1692.

Dr Johnson must have been confident of winning the law suit, for in September 1692, he signed an agreement with the well known carpenter Roger Hurlbut, to partly demolish the property and build a fine town house. The legalities were far from over, but with no problems over money, success seemed in sight.

Dated 1st September 1692, the agreement is fascinating. Roger Hurlbut submitted two designs, one with a balustrade, but Dr Johnson chose the plainer design. This seemed to be in character as the Doctor seemed to be the kind of person who disliked fuss and extravagance.

It would seem that the Johnsons (Ann too appeared to be an extremely capable business woman) drove a hard but fair bargain. All the work was itemised in a precise manner and there were frequent references to work already completed (by Roger Hurlbut?) for Mr Blissett, presumably Joseph Blissett, an Alderman and later Mayor.

The agreement stated that,

BEHIND THE PANELLING THE COMPLICATED HISTORY OF LANDOR HOUSE IS REVEALED. This fascinating photograph provides proof of the existence of a former brick extension (predating Landor House) to the ground floor room on the corner of Chapel Street, now the Headmistress's Study. The thick beam in the centre was from a ship, for it bore identifying markings and to the right a section of lath and plaster wall can be seen. The brick extension to the left had been built long before Roger Hurlbut was engaged to construct Landor House.

"The timber shall be good & sound & well seasoned" and that Hurlbut was "To make a pair of doors ... of good deal with frames of good and sound oake in the same form as Mr Blissetts."

Apart from the outside walls to be constructed from brick and stone and the provision of a new roof with carved cantilevers and cornices, the work to be done was more modification than actual rebuilding. Much of the existing structure was to be retained, especially in the domestic rooms alongside Chapel Street. The kitchen and brewhouse in that wing were to be modified, with rooms being built above.

Three staircases were to be made; the main one leading from the hall, another leading from the side of the kitchen to the rooms above and a third leading from the Doctor's study, near the adjacent cottage, to the garrets.

The ground floor reception rooms were to have transom windows, but the first floor rooms were to have sash windows. The garrets were to have,

"As many luthern windowes ... as the said William Johnson shall see convenient."

The direction to extend and lengthen a parlour nearest to the other cottages,

THE OLDEST PART OF LANDOR HOUSE, AS SEEN FROM CHAPEL STREET.
Probably dating from Medieval times, this wing was used to house kitchens and other domestic
rooms. Much altered internally, many are unaware of the great age of this section of the house.

"Six feet or more into the street equall with the other wing or front of the same
house on the east side,"

seemed to me to be a most interesting detail. Repairs done to the ground floor room
on the corner of Chapel Street clearly indicate how the walls had been extended.

There still exists one massive beam near the entrance to the garrets, at the top of
the second flight of the main stairs. Only part is visible, but it would appear that it
was part of the roof support of the previous building.

Roger Hurlbut was a highly respected local craftsman and he and his brother
William, amongst other work, had refurbished several rooms in Warwick Castle,

THE MAGNIFICENT BANISTER ON THE UPPER LANDING OF LANDOR HOUSE. In the Agreement of 1692, Roger Hurlbut was instructed "To make a stair-case of good sound and well seasoned oake with railes and banisters answerable to it, to lead out of the hall up to the garrets." Today these banisters are a much admired feature, built as they are in a style typical of the late seventeenth century.

including the magnificent Cedar Room. William Hurlbut had rebuilt the Market Hall (now The Museum) in 1670, a building which bore some resemblance to the exterior of Landor House.

Building Commences.

After obtaining a Chancery Decree in 1692 and an award from Sir John Mordaunt in February 1692/3, building actually began in March.

In the agreement, Roger Hurlbut was supposed to complete the building work for £142, with the payments being £10 on September 1st 1692, when the agreement was signed, £100 to be paid in instalments as necessary before the 25th May 1693 and the remaining £32 within a week of the completion of the work.

However, it would appear that Hurlbut went over budget on the house, with eleven dated receipts adding up to a total of £152 7shillings. The first receipt was dated 11th March 1692/3 and the last 17th June. There were also additional receipts, one for £11 paid on 27th June, making a total of £168 8shillings. So not only was Hurlbut over budget, but he was also about a month overtime.

It may have been that there was some sort of disagreement between Johnson and Hurlbut, because the house was not finished according to the signed agreement. In

*THIS MAGNIFICENT OLD BEAM NEAR THE GARRETS IN LANDOR HOUSE
WAS UNDOUBTEDLY PART OF THE ROOF STRUCTURE OF THE PREVIOUS
HOUSE. Perhaps Walter Savage Landor when a boy and numerous other children over the
centuries used it as a seat or played on it. The white hand rails are fairly recent additions to
prevent accidents on the old wooden steps.*

that document, Dr Johnson had stipulated that a study was to be constructed on the
West side, next to Moody's house, with a staircase leading up to the garrets.

However, many years later in 1733, James Fish refers to rooms on that side of the
house as "unfinished." There was a parlour and great chamber unfinished and the
Doctor's Study was on the Chapel Street side of the house, next to the bedroom
above the kitchen.

One way and another, Landor House was extremely costly to Dr Johnson. Even
with the building work costing £168 8sh. that was the smallest expense! The legal
fees amounted to £279 14 9d (plus several hundred pounds for the Chancery
Decree) and £400 was paid for the site and the original houses.

"Armed With Candles We Descended Into the Cellars."

It was difficult to understand why Dr Johnson was so keen to acquire that
particular site. Admittedly it was in an excellent position, with scope for creating a
fine garden, but around one thousand pounds was a great deal of money to spend.
Obviously Dr Johnson was not the sort of character to relish losing a Court Case
once he had decided he wanted to buy the property, but it is interesting to speculate
on his true motives.

We know that the previous house on the site possessed cellars, because these were mentioned in the agreement with Roger Hurlbut. In the seventeenth century, there were a number of secret passages in Warwick and it may well have been that a secret passage existed between St Mary's Church, the Vicarage or the Priory. If he did have Jacobite sympathies, a secret passage might have been very important to Dr Johnson.

That there was an underground passage of some sort is clear from accounts which were carried in "The Book of the Jubilee" produced by the King's High School For Girls in 1929. Three accounts by schoolgirls around 1880, shortly after Landor House had become home to the school, were included in the book.

Miss E. Smith wrote,

"We had an exciting time one morning, exploring the school end of the passage. Armed with candles we descended into the cellars... We went a little distance along the passage and the roots of the trees hung down like creepers."

Also Maud Morin in her account wrote,

"That birthday (Miss Fisher's) was also celebrated by an expedition to the underground passage, under the guidance of Miss Wakefield. The entrance is now altered beyond recognition. I suppose the beginning was merely the house cellar, but there was something deliciously eerie in penetrating to the dark passage, until stopped by fallen stones over which we could peep into a mysterious beyond, that once led all the way to the Priory. For what had it been used in those far off days?"

Some people may dismiss these accounts as fanciful treats for Victorian girls, but I feel sure they are factual accounts. It is perhaps more likely that any secret passage led to St Mary's rather than the Priory, but there may have been several tunnels in the Butts area. At the time of the visit to the passage by some of the senior girls, Miss Fisher and the newly formed Girls' High School were striving to gain credibility. It seems likely that Miss Fisher, coming from a city area, found the passage interesting and wanted the girls to share the experience.

At the present time, there is a section of the cellars under Landor House which is blocked off with relatively new bricks. It seems more than likely that the secret passage explored by the girls was blocked off over one hundred years ago.

Summer 1693. The Johnson Family Move In. Lazy Henry!

There must have been great excitement in that summer of 1693, when nine members of the Johnson family, plus around five servants, moved into the fine new house.

Dr William himself was 50 years old and he must have felt some pride in his achievement, especially after the long fight to gain possession of the site. Ann was 44 and being an efficient organiser, probably relished the challenge in front of her. The ages of the children ranged from 16 to 6 years, so there was plenty of activity!

About a year after moving into Landor House, Dr Johnson fell seriously ill and made out a will. Dated 15th August 1694, almost all the money and property was left to Ann, who was deemed to be an extremely capable person. However, the seven children were to have £400 divided between them, but Henry was threatened with being disinherited because he was,

"Lasy undutifull and wilde."

Parents the world over would recognise this description of a teenager and sympathise with Dr William. Somehow it was comforting to know that even 300 years ago, certain teenagers were a problem!

Digby was obviously his father's favourite as he was to be left his books. Fortunately, the will was never proved and Dr Johnson was to live for another 31 years.

The Great Fire of Warwick.

On September 5th 1694, a terrible fire broke out in Warwick and within five or six hours around 250 of the estimated 600 houses in the town had been destroyed. The fire began opposite to the Lord Leycester Hospital and soon engulfed whole streets and even St Mary's Church.

As the fire raged down Jury Street, Dr Johnson must have been terrified that his fine new house, with its expensive contents, might be destroyed. He had recently bought the timber framed cottages which were actually joined to his house, so the danger was great. He reasoned that if the fire once spread beyond Eastgate, all his property and probably all of Smith Street was doomed.

A graphic description of Dr Johnson's part in the Fire was afterwards given in a petition he wrote for the Fire Court Commissioners on 20th January 1694/5.

"Your Peticoner therefore humbly setts forth—That he att the time of the late dreadful fire, considering the great danger the lower parish was then in and inevitably the same must have been consumed if the house of Mr Heath was not presently pulled down; went to Mr Joseph Blissett, then Mayor of Warwick and told him the same, to which he replyed that he had given orders to have the said house pulled down, butt could gett noe body to doo any thing: Therefore desired and ordered your peticoner to gett men to pull down the same, accordingly he did, tho with much Difficulty and by promising them a reward."

This timber-framed house, which was demolished on the orders of Dr Johnson, was owned by Alderman Heath and let to Nathaniel Gilstrop. Presumably it stood on the corner of Jury Street, just across the town wall from Johnson's cottages.

However, the fire stopped well short of Eastgate, near the site of the present Lord Leycester Hotel and instead of being haled as a hero, Dr Johnson found himself being ordered by the Fire Court to pay £20 compensation (half of what was claimed) to the owner of the demolished property. Could it have been that some of the bitter feelings against Dr Johnson still prevailed?

James Fish the Elder. Parish Clerk.

Over the years, numerous talented and interesting people were frequent visitors to Landor House and none more so than James Fish the Elder.

James Fish was a schoolmaster (perhaps in the old choir school, connected with St Mary's in The Butts) and from 1682 to his death in 1702, he was Parish Clerk of St Mary's. In fact, not only was he Parish Clerk, but he also undertook the duties of Chief Bellringer, Keeper and Transcriber of Records and General Factotum! From 1678, he was connected with the restoration of the Beauchamp Chapel, which had been damaged in 1641 during The Civil War and during the 1690s, he acted as official Keeper of the Chapel at a salary of £2 per year (although this was often not paid). In 1694, he compiled a list of the Beauchamp Chapel Muniments and this document is now in the Bodleian Library in Oxford.

At the time of the Fire of Warwick, James Fish and his family were living in a comfortable house in Church Street, which was entirely destroyed. Some 200 books were lost in the Fire and also some mathematical instruments which were the property of son James, a noted surveyor.

In the political row concerning the Chancery Suit against Rev. Eades, James Fish was heavily implicated, it being alleged that he and his son supported the Vicar by ringing the bells. The Fish family appear to have been deeply religious, always helpful, but desirous of being upwardly mobile! The eldest son, surveyor James born in 1673 and second daughter Mary, born in 1676, were both to be extremely important people in the later life of Ann Johnson.

I have little doubt that in the decade prior to his death, James Fish, the Parish Clerk was a frequent visitor to Landor House as the Johnsons were prominent members of St Mary's congregation and the Johnson and Fish children although of a different social class, were of a similar age.

Rebuilding. Was Dr Johnson Afraid of Another Fire?

The years following the Fire saw the gathering of a large number of skilled builders in Warwick. Not only were many houses needing repair, but St Mary's Church had to be rebuilt.

Francis Smith, a mason architect from Wolverhampton, came to Warwick with his elder brother, to rebuild St Mary's Church and it appeared that the Smith and Fish families became friendly, as James Fish the elder was then the Parish Clerk.

Later Francis Smith became famous and was responsible for many buildings, including the Court House in Warwick. In later life, he and James Fish the younger, being of a similar age, were to be co-trustees of a most important charity. Many houses in Warwick were ordered to replace thatched roofs with tiles in order to minimize the threat of another fire. Many inhabitants were apprehensive. Dr Johnson never had the rooms on the west side of Landor House completed and forty years later, on the death of Ann Johnson, it appeared that the parlour and bedroom on that side were still unfinished, with even the garret above being unused.

Like all disasters, the Great Fire of Warwick must have had a lasting effect on the inhabitants who experienced its horrors. In past ages, plagues, fires and disasters were more common, but deep traumatic effects may still have been felt by the populace.

With no insurance in those times, cautious Dr Johnson may have felt safer with an unfinished parlour lacking wooden panelling adjoining the neighbouring property.

A Funeral and a Wedding At St Mary's.

Around four years after the Johnson family moved into Landor House, tragedy struck and son Digby died at the age of 17. This must have been a terrible blow for the family, especially for Dr William, as it was clear that Digby was his favourite son. Twenty eight years later, when Dr Johnson himself died, in his will he asked to be buried as near as possible to Digby. This seemed such a sad request and it indicated that like so many other bereaved parents, he never quite forgot the grief he felt when Digby died.

There are no details of what caused Digby's death, but on 24th May 1697, Landor House must have been a very sad place, after poor Digby had been buried in St Mary's Church.

A few years later, in October 1701, a happy family occasion took place when 19 years old Ursula Johnson married the splendidly named Musgrave Heighington in St Mary's Church.

It is interesting to speculate on the state of Landor House on that day. Presumably Ursula wore a white satin suit (mentioned in later lists) such as was fashionable at the time. Perhaps Ursula rode to St Mary's Church in the family chariot, suitably cleaned and decorated for the occasion. Maybe however, she walked to the church like some of the guests.

Doubtless, the main parlour and withdrawing room (now the Headmistress's study) was used for a celebratory meal and gathering after the happy event.

The newly weds must have remained in Warwick, perhaps even staying in Landor House. Just over a year later, Ursula gave birth to a daughter Mary and the first grandchild must have brought Dr William and Ann Johnson much happiness.

Business Matters.

In 1697, Dr Johnson was obliged to travel to Ireland when his father died, for there were many problems concerning his inheritance. Although the Doctor's mother was in agreement, a brother and cousin began legal proceedings contesting the inheritance. The estates which William inherited were 219 acres near Lisburn in County Down, close to the important River Lagan.

The route to Ireland was via Liverpool, there embarking on a ship which might take many hours to make the crossing. Dr Johnson had several relations in Liverpool, but the journey must have been very difficult. So when in 1700 it was necessary for him to travel again, this time he stayed over a year, until matters were sorted out satisfactorily.

Eventually, the Irish estates were leased to various tenants, the rents being forwarded to Warwick via agents. However there was frequent trouble in after years concerning the payment of the rents and the idea of the Doctor as an absentee landlord, must have angered many of the Irish members of the family.

If the Johnsons were alive today, they would probably have a bulging filing cabinet or a suitably programmed home computer, holding domestic details, besides essential notes connected with a medical practice. It seemed as if Dr William was always anticipating future legal action as rough drafts of letters, as well as important legal documents, were carefully preserved in boxes.

The Johnsons were wise to anticipate legal proceedings for during their time in Warwick they were involved in numerous law suits. James Wright, as lawyer to the Johnsons (possibly the only attorney in Warwick) had a lucrative position, which brought in much money over many years.

A long standing argument was the boundary dispute with Martha Rogers, who owned a house in The Butts, the garden of which adjoined the Johnsons' orchard. It would appear that water from Mrs Roger's house caused flooding in the Johnson's orchard, which was especially awkward when the Parish officials carried out the ceremony of Beating the Bounds, once a year. The boundary line between the Parishes of St Mary and St Nicholas passed through the Johnsons' land (then through the cottage nearest to Eastgate!) and repairs were frequently necessary to the path.

James Fish the surveyor who became very friendly with the Johnsons, wrote a memorandum on the subject and I hope it amuses you as much as it amused me!

"Mrs Rogers bought a Garden or peece of land of one Mr Cawthorn on which before the great fire at Warwick stood a poore little cottage house. The sd peece of ground was about 37 yards long and 8 yards broad and is fenced on the North side with the neighbours hedg and on the South side with Mrs Rogers own hedg... When Mrs Rogers built her house upon the sd ground Dr Johnston gave her leave to set her house and garden pales to the outside of her ground and accordingly Mrs Rogers chose one workman and Dr Johnston chose another to set out the same justly betwixt them both.

... But since Mrs Rogers has made a pump to serve her house with water instead of making a way to carry the overplus water into the street or by gutters to carry the same otherways into her own ground as all other neighbours do she or her tenants have made or caused to be made a gutter through her garden wall into Mrs Johnstons orchard... Mrs Johnston has been obliged to lay lathers and boards over the sd washed ground for the Parishioners to goe their usual walk upon... all at her own charge.

Yet Mrs Rogers tenants or their servants do still continually pour down all their water and filth into Mrs Johnstons orchard contrary to all equity and justice."

This boundary dispute was very long running and in 1730 arguments still continued. As the years went by the arguments grew more serious with talk of water running into Mrs Rogers' stable muckhill and later into the Johnstons's straw pit. "Things do not change much," commented a historian, but then neither does human nature! If this dispute occurred today, doubtless some T.V. "sitcom" writer would base a comedy series on it.

How The Johnson Family Lived.

We know much about the kind of lives the Johnsons led thanks to various lists compiled by James Fish after the death of Ann Johnson.

It would appear that the house was largely self sufficient as to food. Until I read the inventory of the various rooms, I had no idea that a house of this size would have had a dairy, brew-house, hen house and pig sty. It was a complete eye-opener to me, especially as there were horses and cows also. The ground behind the house and cottages must have resembled a mini-farm, with ducks, pigeons and dogs adding to the chaos! No wonder Dr Johnson found it necessary to rent a field at nearby Bridge End (Tythe Close, together with barn for £9 10sh. a year) at one time.

Besides all the livestock, much fruit was grown in the orchard. Apples, grapes, elderberries, walnuts and strawberries were mentioned, so it sounded as if the excess water made the fruit thrive!

From the other details of food, it sounded as if the Johnsons were very wealthy, as tea, coffee and chocolate were drunk; all of those items being very expensive in the Eighteenth Century. Beer and perhaps wine was bottled as nine dozen quart bottles were mentioned in one list.

The furniture in the house is itemised so clearly in the following list there is no need for further comment from me. I hope you enjoy trying to visualize each room and finding examples of similar pieces in antique books just as I did.

An Inventory of all the Household Goods that were left at Mrs Johnstons by Agreement with Mr Willes after he had taken the same upon the 27th day of September 1733.

The Brewhouse
One large copper Furnace valued at − £6 15sh.

One Lesser copper furnace at – £2 5sh.
One Great Mashing Tub at – 6sh.
Two Long Wooden Spouts – 3sh.
One Old Table and Plate Rack – 1sh.

The Pantry
Dressers and shelfs
One cupboard or safe – 3sh
One wooden Skreen Tinned – 2sh 6d

The Kitchen
Dressers shelfs and Bacon Rack – 5sh.
Six Large Pewter dishes weighing sixty five pound at 8d
    per pound – £2 3sh 4d
The Fire Grate and cheeks, the fender and Two Great Racks,
One Hearth Grate at 5d per pound
    The Gibbet, Rack & Links at 3d per pound – £2
    The Jack and Stone Weight – 15sh
Two large spits – 5sh
Two other spits and Eight Bird Spits – 6sh.
Window shutters
One Large & one lesser Ironing boards – 2sh
One Large Salt box – 2sh.
One Forme and two little wooden stooles – 1sh.
One Square Table next the stoves – 1sh.

Little Room next the Kitchen
One Round Table – 6sh
One Elbow and four other Cain chaires – 6sh.
One couch – 1sh 6d
Fire Grate, One Fire Shovel, Tonges and Fender – 3sh
One Old Pair of Bellows and hand brush – 1sh 6d
Two straw Fire Skreens – 4d
The Chimney peece Picture – 2sh 6d
Twelve other Little prints – 2sh
Window Shutters
Window Curtains Vallions and Rod – 2sh 6d
The Tapestry Hangings – £1 1sh
The Closset Nine shelfs

The Withdrawing Roome
One Slate Table – 3sh
One Elbow & six other Cain chaires – 10sh 6d
Six red velvet cushions – 12sh.

One Looking Glass – £1 1sh
Two Glass Schonces – 4sh
Two hand Fireskreens – 6d
One Pair of Dogs – 2sh
Window Shutters, Window Curtains, Vallions and Rod – 2sh
The Hangings – 15sh

The Parlour
One Black Card Table – 2sh
One corner Table – 6sh.
One Great Looking Glass – £1 16sh
Six Glass schonces – 10sh 6d
One clock and clock case – £5
One broken weather Glass – 4sh 6d
The Fire Grate with Brass Faces – 10sh
The Fender, Fire shovel and Tonges – 2sh
Two hand Fire skreens – 6d
Eight Kain chaires – 12sh
The chimney Peece Picture – £1 1sh
The Drs and Mrs Johnstons Pictures – £2 2sh
Miss Heyingtons Picture – £1 1sh
Sr John Bowyers and two other Pictures – 8sh
Eight yellow silk cushions – 8sh
Two yellow silk window seats – 2sh
Window shutters and Iron barrs

The Hall
One Great Ovall Table – 14sh
One square Table – 4sh
Two Long Formes – 3sh
Six wooden schonces – 1sh
One Old Lanthorn – 2sh
The Fire Grate – 3sh 6d

Little Roome at the Yard steps
One candle coffer one dresser 3 shelfs

The Unfinished Parlour

The Dairy
Two Trussells, a table Leaf and one long shelf – 3sh 6d

Back Kitchen
Long dresser one Iron crow
Two coffee Roasters – 2sh

Little Room
One square table – 1sh
Six shelfs and corner cupboard
One forme

The Larder.
One salting tub and cover and settle
One Varges barrell and settle – 2sh 6d
One hanging shelf

Hen House.
Old Bricks and quarrys
One old Hen Pen

Coale House
The Scales beam and weights one being half a hundred and four others
    weights being another half hundred – 14sh

The Court.
One larg Leaden cistern – £3 10sh

Grainery
One wheelbarrow, one strike, Two Wilmcot stones about 3 feet
    square – 5sh
Two large window frames – 2sh 6d
About 300 of new good bricks.

Coach House.
One charriot

Stables
One iron rake and fork and coffer – 1sh 6d

Hogsty
One wooden and two stone troughs – 3sh

Barn.
Three old ladders – 3sh

Garden
One stone Rowler and two long forms. — 9sh
in the sumer house one forme

The Maids Chamber
One bedstead and brown furniture lined — 7sh 6d
One Feather bed and two bolsters weighing 85 pounds at 6d per
  pound — £2 2sh 6d
One old blanket and rug — 1sh
One other Bedstead curtains & matt — 5sh
One Great Chest — 10sh
One Fire Grate — 1sh
Window shutters and 2 old chaires — 4sh
The Hangings.

Store Roome
One Hanging shelf and a forme.

Kitchen Chamber.
One bedstead & Green Curtains lined and Counterpaine — £2
One Feather bed one Bolster and two pillows weighing 107 pounds at
  10 pence a pound — £4 7sh 6d
Two Blankets — 7sh 6d
One Easie chaire and cushion — 10sh 6d
Three Old Kaine chairs — 6sh
Four Green cushions — 5sh
One Square Table and Drawer — 2sh
One Scrutone under the clock — 16sh
The Eight Day clock — £7
One Great Skrew tone wallnut — £2
One Little Hand board — 6d
Grate, Fender, fireshovel and Tonges and Poker — 11sh 6d
One Paire of Bellows — 1sh 6d
One Close stoole and Pewter Pan — 2sh 6d
The Chimney Peece Picture — 8sh.
Tapestry Hangings — £2
Window Curtains and Shutters — 5sh

The Study
One Large Hanging Press and 2 drawers — £1 10sh
One Good Chest of Drawers — 12sh
One Large square Table — 4sh
One Lesser square Table and drawers — 2sh 6d

Two Chaires – 6d

Passage
Miss Johnstons four Pictures – £1
Fourteen Little Pictures – 1sh 2d
The Bell, Lines and roles – 2sh 6d
One Movable shelf.

Miss Heyingtons Roome
One Bedstead and Brown Furniture lined with callicoe – £1 10sh
One Feather Bed Bolster and 2 pillows weighing 80 pounds at 9d
    per pound – £3
Two Blankets and a Counterpain – 4sh
Two Old Kaine Chaires – 2sh
One Couch with Squab and Pillows – 7sh 6d
The Fire grate and Tongs – 2sh 8d
Window Shutters and Iron Barr.

Corner Chamber
One Bedstead of chambler Furniture lined with yellow silk & Quilt the
    same – £2
One Feather Bed, Bolster and 2 pillows weighing 115 pounds at 9d
    per pound – £3 16sh 8d
Two Blankets – 5sh
The Hangings – £1 6sh
Two Sets of Window curtains, vallions & rods – 9sh
One Elbow chair and Cushion – 1sh 3d
Four Kaine Chair and one Close stoole chair – 5sh
Six Yellow silk cushions – 3sh 6d
One Corner Cupboard – 3sh 6d
One Chest of Drawers – £1 5sh
The Window Table & Stands and Dressing box – 7sh
One Great Glass – 18sh
Two Glass Schonces – 3sh
One very Good Bowrow (Bureau?) – £1 7sh 6d
One Fire grate – 8sh
The Fender, Fire shovell and Tongs and Poker and dogs – 6sh 6d
One Pair of Bellows and Brush – 1sh
Four white Figures and one yellow figure on the mantle peece
The Chimney Peece Picture – 8sh

The Closset
One Black Table and Drawer – 1sh

Three Old Chairs and One worked chair − 1sh 6d
Pictures Five Kings and Queens − 2sh 6d
One, the offering to our Saviour− 1sh
The Boyes and Deaths Head − 1sh
One worked Peece over the Doore − 2sh
And about 20 or 30 other Lesser Pictures − 2sh 6d

Little Dark Chamber
One Half headed Bedstead & curtains − 5sh
One Feather Bed and Bolster weighing 85 pounds
at 7d per pound - £2 9sh 7d
Two Blanketts and a Rug − 1sh
One Square Table − 2sh 6d
One old chaire

Best Chamber
One wrought Bed lined with satin and the quilt the same − £12 7sh 6d
One Downe Bed, Bolster and 2 Pillows weighing 82 pounds at 18d
  per pound − £6 3sh
One Pair of Blanketts − 10sh
One Mattress Quilted − 15sh
Six black Kain Chairs − 18sh
Six yellow satin cushions − 12sh
Two Green Tabby cushions − 5sh
Two Blew satin cushions − 5sh
One Wrought cushion − 2sh
Two black matted Elbow chaires − 1sh
One Cedarwood cabbinet − £1 10sh
Two Setts of Green Window curtains vallions and Rods − 9sh
One Square Table and Drawer − 5sh
One Looking Glass − 16sh
Two Glass Schonces − 3sh
One Copper Tea Kettle Lampe & Stand − 12sh
One Twigen Fire skreen − 4sh
One Tea Table − 2sh
Fire Grate
One Brass Hearth and Fire shovell and Tonges − 12sh
One pair of Bellows − 1sh
One Floore Carpet − 12sh
One Close stoole and Pewter Pan − 2sh 6d
Three coloured and two white alabaster figures
The Tapestry Hangings − £3

Chimney Peece Picture one sacrifice and three other
Little Pictures – 5sh 6d

The Great Unfinished Chamber
One deale Box of Beds feet and sash lines
One Deale Ladder ⎫
One Old Trunk and 3 boards ⎭ 3 shillings

The Dairy Chamber
One Bedstead and Blew curtains – 15sh
One Feather Bed Bolster and 2 Pillows weighing 83 pounds at 9d
    per pound – £3 2sh 6d
Two old Blankets and a quilt – 5sh
One Elbow Kain chaire and cushion
    and Two other worked chaires – 4sh
One Table and Stand – 5sh
The Fire Grate Fire shovel and Tonges – 3sh
The Tapestry Hangings – 10sh
Window Curtains – 2sh
Window Shutters

Staircase First Flight
Thirteen Framed Pictures – £1 6sh
Twenty unframed Pictures – 3sh 4d
Solomans Picture – 5sh

The Gallery
One Large Map of the World – 5sh
Three Lackerd Framed Pictures – 7sh 6d
Eleven Lesser Framed pictures – 1sh 3d
Fifteen unframed Pictures

Staircase Upper Flight
The Weather Glass – 3sh
Eleven Little Framed pictures – 1sh
Twenty unframed Pictures 2 Maps – 3sh

Nurserie Garret
One Bedstead and Brown Curtains lined with white – £1
One Feather bed and One Feather Pillow weighing 83 pounds
    at 7d per pound – £2 8sh 5d
One large Flock Pillow – 1sh

Three Old Blankets − 1sh
One Little Couch and Squab − 2sh
Two Old Kaine Chaires − 6d
The Grate, Fender, Fireshovel & Tonges − 5sh 6d

Middle Garret
The Drying lines and one Casement

Corner Garret
One Old Bedstead and Old couch

Thomass Chamber
One Old Bedstead and Bed mat

The Further Chamber

October the 10th 1733

Then the above written Account was examined and allowed to be a True Inventorie
    by me William Harrison
Received the 21th day of December 1734 of Tho. Archer Esq by the hands of Mr John Hall the sum of One hundred and twenty five pounds in full for all the said Household Goods then left in the house as above mentioned except the Dressers shelfs window shutters and pictures.
    I say received by me James Fish

Sheer Luxury!

The contents of the best bedroom (presumably Ann and Dr William's own) struck me as being luxurious by any standards. Even today, down beds, satin quilts, ten satin cushions and a mirror in the carpeted room, would be considered extremely comfortable. Tea making facilities in bedrooms are still not standard in many hotels.

With a servant to attend to the coal fire and a close stool in case it was needed, I think I could have lived quite happily in that room!

The Death of Dr Johnson.

In November 1725, Dr William died aged 82. It was a great age and a quiet funeral at St Mary's Church was requested.

In his will, he left everything to his wife Ann, except a few personal bequests and some money to the poor. Daughter Ursula was to receive 20 guineas a year and daughter Ann (then Mrs Griffin) 10 guineas, but there was an addition 'if alive'

DR WILLIAM JOHNSON 1643–1725.
This portrait shows the Doctor in his red robes as a Fellow of the Royal College of Physicians in
London. His books and a skull (which appears to have laurel leaves sprouting from the back) can
be seen in the background.

Simon Photography, Leamington Spa.

ANN JOHNSON 1648–1733.
With her long, light-brown hair, complete with flower decoration, Ann's face looks surprisingly modern.
Her bluish-green dress with rose-pink motifs is lined at the sleeves and elsewhere with rose-pink satin. Lace can be seen at the neckline and below the sleeves.
An educated and sensible woman, Ann had a great impact on the history of Warwick by leaving all her assets, including Landor House, to a Charitable Trust.

Simon Photography, Leamington Spa.

THE BABY PORTRAIT IN LANDOR LIBRARY. *A painted caption underneath claims that it is a likeness of "The only son of Dr and Mrs Johnston" but this would seem unlikely. The meticulous James Fish merely listed it as "The Chimney Peece Picture" in the Inventory of 1733 and he knew the three Johnson sons well. Perhaps it is a secret Jacobite painting — inferring the Royal parentage of James Francis Edward (The Old Pretender) by the King Charles spaniel and crown of laurel leaves? Such paintings were common in the latter years of the seventeenth century, when open support for the deposed King James 11 and his son would have been most unwise.*

Simon Photography, Leamington Spa

DID THE TWO BLANK PANELS ONCE HOLD THE JOHNSON PORTRAITS? The measurements of the portraits of William and Ann Johnson are exactly the same as the blank panels on either side of the Baby portrait, which is set above the fireplace. Now in the first floor room above the Hall in Landor House, it would appear that at some time, the whole section of panelling was removed from the Parlour on the ground floor. The open door on the right leads to the main landing and it would seem that this room was once the "Best Chamber" in the time of the Johnsons.

suggesting the family saw nothing of her. Granddaughter Mary was left 5 shillings and so was son Henry, which suggests that his father thought no more of him than he had done years ago! In the absence of other bequests, it appeared that the other children were already dead.

Five pounds was to be paid to both St Mary's and St Nicholas' Church for distribution amongst the poor on Christmas Day. A similar sum was to be paid to each church for distribution on Christmas Day, the following year. Traditionally, Christmas Day was the time when charity was given to the poor, so the choice of day is not surprising. At that time, five pounds was a decent sum for the poor, with a largish loaf costing 2d.

The legal controversy which had pursued William in life, continued long after his death. Poor Ann Johnson had to wait for four years, whilst lawsuits were settled and in the end the legal fees amounted to £500.

Family Portraits.

Portraits of both William and Ann Johnson were set into the panelling of the main parlour. In 1877, when Landor House was handed over to the King's School Foundation, they were removed and suitably framed.

THE RETURN OF THE PORTRAITS OF WILLIAM AND ANN JOHNSON IN MAY 1954. Removed from Landor House in 1877, for many years the portraits hung in the Court House. On the occasion of the 75th Anniversary of The King's High School For Girls, The Mayor of Warwick, Mr E. G. Tibbits, returned the portraits to the Headmistress Miss F. W. Hare. (W.C.R.O.)

For many years they hung in the Assembly Rooms in the Court House, but in May 1954, they were handed back to the King's High School For Girls by Mr E.G. Tibbits, then Mayor, on the 75th anniversary of the founding of the Girls' School.

One portrait still remains in the panelling in Landor House, now in the main first floor room, overlooking Smith Street. It is clear that the portraits of William and Ann Johnson were once set into the panelling either side of this remaining portrait. In all probability, the entire section of panelling was removed from the main parlour on the ground floor, possibly in the late eighteenth century.

The remaining portrait is that of a baby and the painted caption underneath states that the baby was the only son of Dr and Ann Johnson and he died unmarried.

James Fish knew the Johnson family extremely well, and although he listed the other portraits in the Inventory of 1733, not so this one. Had it been a family portrait, there was no way he would have been ignorant of the fact.

Further mystery surrounds the Baby painting as it appears that an extra cloth has been added in green paint, presumably to cover up the baby's bottom! Was this done in prudish Victorian times? It is said that Miss Lea, the second Headmistress of the King's High School, disliked the painting and had it covered up in 1896. It was only rediscovered in the later nineteen forties.

The Cottages In the Time of the Johnsons.

When Dr Johnson purchased the remaining cottages from Edward Heath (the document was dated 30th June and the money was to be paid before 29th September) he paid £140. For some years, the Moody family had been leasing the property, which the Heath family bought merely as an investment. Dr Johnson wanted the use of the ground behind the cottages, which gave more space for orchards and gardens. Also the cottages were still actually joined to Landor House at roof level and elsewhere.

In 1694, Bridget Moody was allowed to stay on as tenant of the property, at a rent of £6 per year, but from the onset the Johnsons retained the use of the extra ground.

In 1708, Francis Dod, an innkeeper took the lease of the cottages and turned the premises into "The Nag's Head"—one of many inns in Warwick at that time. Careful Dr Johnson had several tough clauses included in the lease. Not only was Dod to keep the pales and gates in good repair, but if he fell behind with the rent, after 14 days, the property could be repossessed. Also Dr Johnson was given the right to inspect any repairs or alterations, access being given to him at any time during the day.

In those days, the yard between the cottages and the town wall and Eastgate was much larger than today and there was room for a number of outbuildings, in which to house horses and coaches. With the cottages now so quiet, it is difficult to picture a scene with steaming horses, mugs of ale and bawdy songs!

After a few years, the inn was given the more up-market name of the "Coach and Horses". After the death of William, Ann Johnson let the inn to Thomas Bolton, at an annual rent of £11 10shillings.

ANN JOHNSON'S CHARITY

"A few years before she dyed she told me that She would give all her Estate to charitable uses. And that I should be one of her trustees. And she would have me come as often as I could to advise her about the same."

So wrote James Fish a short time after Ann Johnson's death.

Lonely and Worrying Days.

No sooner had 77 year old Ann Johnson got over the death of her husband, than life dealt another cruel blow. A few months after the death of her father poor Ursula, aged only 45, died and was buried at St Mary's Church on August 12th 1726. Prior to her death she may well have been living in Landor House and it seems likely that her husband was already dead. Ursula's daughter Mary was not mentioned again, except that the small panelled room next to the Corner bedroom was listed in 1733 as being "Miss Heyington's Room". After Ursula's death, it may well have been that Mary visited her grandmother occasionally, using that room when she did so. At no time did James Fish mention the grandaughter's presence, so she probably died long before Ann Johnson herself.

Alone, except for two or three resident servants, Ann Johnson relied more and more on visits from James Fish, the surveyor, who acted as manager for the properties. James' unmarried sister Mary and another friend Mary Simmonds, often acted as companions to Ann Johnson, sometimes staying overnight in Landor House.

With a considerable estate, comprising of the two houses in Warwick and land in Northern Ireland, Ann needed help and James Fish proved the ideal person. Without the integrity of James, there may well have been no Ann Johnson Charity and the poor of Warwick over several centuries would have lost out. With no close family to help her, elderly Ann Johnson was in a most vulnerable position.

Disagreements With Her Lawyer.

For many years James Wright and his family, as the chief (only?) legal firm in Warwick had done much business with the Johnsons. The numerous law suits and the high fees involved had meant that they were very lucrative clients.

However, Ann Johnson became very angry when no money was forthcoming from the Irish estates. By 1730, the law suits with Dr Johnson's brother, cousin and tenant were all satisfactorily completed and Ann was anxious to know exactly what money she had, so that she could make out her will and set up a Charity Trust to benefit the poor of Warwick.

Perhaps rich, elderly widows have always been considered easy prey for the unscrupulous, but capable Ann Johnson became quite determined she would not be duped. After many requests from her, Attorney James Wright had sent letters to the Irish agent of her property, but no money or precise valuations materialised.

In an age when bribery was common, it may well have been that certain members of the Johnson family in Ireland were bribing the agent in Dublin to employ delaying tactics, in the hope that Ann would die intestate. After all, she had no family living in Warwick and at 81, could not be expected to live for long.

When Ann Johnson heard a rumour that lawyer James Wright had been mocking her in public, saying,

> "Poor woman, she makes a noise of giving all her estates to charitable uses, alas what will she have to give?"

her patience finally snapped! During the final year of her life, she severed connections with James Wright, removing her documents from his care. Apparently she feared that after her death, the lawyer might claim her property in lieu of legal fees connected with the Irish estates and she asked James Fish to help her draw up a will and Trust Deed for the proposed Charity.

James Fish had been Churchwarden at St Mary's in 1730 and 1731 and as such he would have been responsible for doling out much of the charity then available. In many ways he was an ideal person to give advice and he seemed to be as keen as Ann Johnson herself to organise a Charity Trust. It would appear that 59 year old James had little to gain himself from the organisation of such a scheme, but the power, responsibility and increased status of being named Chief Trustee probably appealed to him.

Greed does bring out the worst in characters and throughout history, there are tales of opposition from covetous people, whenever it is proposed to leave money to charity. However 83 year old Ann was determined to leave her money as she wished—to the underprivileged of the town she loved.

So Ann Johnson's will and Trust Deed was drawn up in early 1732/3 (until 1752, the New Year began on Lady Day 25th March according to the Julian Calendar and dates in January, February and early March were usually written with both numbers) but James Fish had the good sense to realise the documents needed to be worded by a professional lawyer. James persuaded Ann to allow him to show the proposals to lawyer James Wright, who was to be instructed to draw up the necessary legal documents. Naturally there was much ill feeling on both sides and as Ann by this time was incapable of reading the documents herself, she refused to sign until James Fish had had a chance to check all the wording.

The Trust Deed was worked out sensibly, so that poor ancient or other needy persons of the Parishes of St Mary and St Nicholas would benefit. Besides James

Fish, who was named as Chief Trustee, Francis Smith, the respected architect builder and Doctor Bree, presumably Ann Johnson's own doctor, were named as Co-Trustees.

The Will and Trust Deed were signed on 5th and 6th March 1732/3 and only just in time, for Ann Johnson died about a month afterwards.

"She Dyed About Midnight."

The scene is not difficult to imagine as James Fish gave graphic descriptions in his numerous notes.

The 84 year old widow, bedridden and nearly blind, lay propped up on the feather pillows of her four poster bed, its thick hangings partially drawn. The best bedroom, crowded with quality furniture, fashionable about fifty years previously, was lit only by a couple of candles and the flickering flames of the coal fire, which burned constantly in the grate. Ann Sabin, the long-serving housekeeper, and Mary Fish would have been asked to leave the room, whilst a most important final ceremony took place—the handing over of a well-worn key. Besides James Fish, only Dr Bree was present.

To allow James Fish to narrate the events himself ...

> "She gave me more pticular direction ... and at last after she had given me an account of her chief treasure ... she gave me the key of the same."

This was virtually the last thing Ann ever did for two days later,

> "On 4th April 1733 she dyed about midnight... And next morning I sent to Dr Bree who came and then we opened the will and we together did search find out and take account of the great part of the chief treasure."

Keep Those Doors Locked!

James Fish went to some lengths to explain how he had asked his sister Mary to stay with Ann Johnson, right to the end. Afterwards, Mary locked all the doors, locking the keys themselves in a drawer until the morning.

After James Fish and Dr Bree had found the treasure, the doors were locked again, as the Doctor was obliged to travel to Coventry. Being entrusted with the keys to Landor House, James was ultra-careful and he wrote,

> "I did keep the keys at my own house and did not myself nor would suffer any other person to goo up the stairs there all the day."

James Fish took his responsibilities so seriously at times, it was laughable, but better that than have goods or money stolen.

The following day, all three trustees went to Landor House.

"We made further search and when we had done and lockt up the doors we lockt up all the keys in a box to which we have every one a key which can not be unlockt unless all the three keys be brought together."

As a Churchwarden three years previously, James Fish would have observed the advantages of the Parish Chest, with the statutory three locks. Being an ultra cautious man in many respects, as Chief Trustee he thought the idea worth copying.

The Funeral.

Wise Ann Johnson had insisted that James Fish be the custodian of her will and after her death, the Trustees took the will to the lawyer for advice on how to proceed. Feeling that he had been snubbed or branded dishonest, James Wright, not surprisingly, was distinctly uncooperative. Eventually he and Richard Wright did process the documents, but they took their time and James Wright never lost an opportunity to make life difficult for Mr Fish.

Ann Johnson had left precise instructions as to her funeral and the list of expenses makes interesting reading.

Paid Ed. Williams for the 2 wooden coffins & other work £4 11sh.
Paid Rob Grey for the leaden coffin − £7 2sh.
Paid Sam Wright for opening the vault − 8sh.
Paid Clerk of St Mary's for the burial dues − £1 17sh 6d
Paid Clerk of St Nich Parish dues − 5sh.
Paid Mrs Rogers for wine for the funeral − £1 9sh 6d
Paid Mrs Boddington for the maid servants mourning − £4 10sh
Paid Mr Smith for the man servants cloth − £3 8sh 3d
Paid Mr Paris for the brass plate for the coffin − £1 10sh
Paid Mr Dadleys bill for the funeral charges − £33 7sh.

With a bill of over £57, it was an expensive interment. Like her husband Ann was buried in St Mary's Church, inside three coffins, the innermost being lead. Also on top of this, there was the sum of £33 4sh for the erection of a marble monument in the church. (This total also included a marble chimney piece in the house and a marble stone set upon the vault).

This memorial to Dr William and Ann Johnson can still be seen in St Mary's Church. However in recent times it has been moved from the North Transept to the wall facing the Beauchamp Chapel. The inscription, planned by Dr William, is in Latin and the memorial is now placed about 30 feet above floor level. Some church guides now carry binoculars, which are very useful in such cases!

The Charity Trust and Will.

In her will, Ann Johnson decreed that all her personal belongings were to be sold for the best price which could be obtained and her houses rented out. The profits, after deduction of money for expenses and repairs, were to be used to help the poor of Warwick. Also money was to be used in placing poor children of both or either sex as apprentices and later in helping them set up in their respective trades.

One of the features of the Charity was that each Trustee was to be allocated an equal share of the profits to dole out privately, as he saw fit. Of course each Trustee had to account for the sums of money and copies of the accounts were to be readily available for inspection at both of the churches. (The only two in Warwick at that time).

In addition to the main fund, there was a sum set aside as "Bread Money" for each parish. Each year, £2 12sh was to be paid to a baker who was to send 6 twopenny loaves each Sunday, to be distributed to 6 poor persons. In St Mary's Church, there are still bread shelves bearing the name of Mrs Johnson.

The only condition was that any recipients of the charity were to be communicants of the Church of England. In those times, this would have been a perfectly reasonable condition as all Roman Catholics and Non-Conformists were still regarded with great suspicion.

In the first half of the eighteenth century, there were many charitable trusts set up as new ideas meant an awakening of a social conscience. Many better off people thought that if the poor were educated, it would help to prevent mischief, vagrancy and idleness! Ann Johnson must have been impressed by the Charity School set up over nearby Eastgate and having no immediate family (there was no further mention of the grandaughter) setting up a charity trust seemed the kind and sensible thing to do.

There were other kind acts in Ann's will and these included legacies of £20 each to Mary Fish and Mary Simmonds and £5 each to the three Trustees of the Charity, Dr Bree, Francis Smith and James Fish. The wayward son Henry (if living) was left 5 shillings on top of the 5 shillings left him by his father! Ann Johnson even made the provision that Henry was to make no further claim on her estate.

The faithful housekeeper Ann Sabin was left £5 and all the servants were left a year's wages on top of what was owed to them. When I read in an account book that Ann Sabin had been paid only £7 17sh for her legacy and wages in full, I thought she had been swindled, until I discovered that at that time, female live-in servants were paid less than £3 per year very often! A payment to Hannah Bramwell, the other resident servant, of only £2 17sh, confirmed the low annual wages then paid.

Sorting Out Begins.

After the funeral, the enormous task of sorting and pricing the contents of the house began. James Fish did almost all of the sorting as he knew the house better than anyone and was also Chief Trustee. James was able to give the Charity almost all his time, whereas Dr Bree and Francis Smith often had other business to attend to.

On 20th April 1733, just a few weeks after the death of Ann Johnson, James reached his 60th birthday. By no manner of means a young man, he had an enormous task in front of him. Anyone who has ever had to dispose of a deceased person's house will realise the difficulties of the situation, which was complicated by the fact that the Trustees had sworn on oath, amongst other things, to obtain the best price possible for all items.

The task of the Trustees, James Fish in particular, was hampered by the continued antagonism of James Wright, the lawyer. There was certainly a clash of personalities, but each appeared to mistrust the other. The two men seemed to respect each other as professionals, yet would do everything possible to anger the other.

The Stolen Milk Barrels!

One of the first things sorted out was the lease of some Park ground, which may have been near Bridge End. It appeared that James Wright bought the lease, together with a hay rick and carts, for a lower price than Dr Bree would have paid later. So James Fish felt that the Charity had been deprived of at least £20 as a result.

About 10 days after this, when James Fish was elsewhere, James Wright sent his servant to Landor House to collect several milk barrels from one of the outhouses. The messenger told the servants at Landor House that Dr Bree had ordered them to be collected. Of course, Dr Bree said he had no knowledge of any of it and when he discovered the loss of the barrels, James Fish was incensed. He said he had not even had time to price them!

When reading of this occurrence, it struck me that the barrels may have been taken as a prank against James Fish, who seemed to take all his duties so seriously. I could just imagine others in the town laughing their heads off at such an escapade!

No doubt James Wright would have said that the barrels were part of the farm equipment, in his opinion and therefore they already belonged to him. However James Fish did not forget this episode and for months was mentioning it in the various notes he wrote concerning Ann Johnson's affairs.

The Contents of Landor House Sold.

For weeks and months, it seemed that James Fish did little else but sort out the belongings of the Johnson family. The sixty year old surveyor must have had little time to pursue his own career, for he spent most days in Landor House, listing the treasure, documents and household goods.

Within weeks of Ann Johnson's death, certain items were sold, when a reasonable offer was received, but most things were listed, priced by experts (mostly shopkeepers such as Mrs Jones and Mrs Simmonds, who priced the clothes and linen) and reserved for the house sales. Most of these took place during June and July.

It appeared that only serious buyers, who were given special notification, attended and it is interesting to imagine Landor House, with hundreds of items laid out for sale, like a genteel jumble sale! In our throw-away age, it is difficult to appreciate how much used items were valued, before mass production made clothes and household items more plentiful and affordable.

The following is a list of some of the more interesting items.

> Mr York bought a chassing dish and spitting pot for 1sh 9d
> Mrs Casemore paid £2 14sh for 41 hundred of hay at 16p per hundred.
> A lignum Vitae Mortar & pestel was bought for 4 shillings
> Chiurgeens case of instruments was bought for 12sh 6d
> A lancet case & scissors was sold for 2 shillings.
> 9 dozen quart bottles were bought for 9 shillings.
> Rec. of Dr Bree for six pound of sugar − 3 sh.
> Rec. of Mrs Simmonds for 14 pound of old filthy feathers 4sh
> Rec. of Mrs Bolton for 28 pounds of chese − 5sh 10d
> Rec. of Mrs Duncumin for 3 childs Flannell mantles − 3 sh
> Rec. of Mrs Willmot for one pair of sheets − 7sh.
> Rec. of Mrs Norton for one silk handkerchief − 2sh.
> Rec. of Mrs Hanah Tommas for spectacles and case − 8d
> Rec. of Mrs Taylor for a pot and marum − 6d
> Rec. of Mr Richd Smith for marum and an orange tree − 1sh 3d
> Rec. of Mrs Bradley for an old napkin press − 2sh 6d
> Rec. of her for a horse to dry cloths on − 2sh
> Rec. of Mrs Smiths maid for an old calamanco gown & ribbons − 10sh
> Rec. of Mr Lydiots maid for 8 shifts − 17sh.

The lists were endless and included a marvellous picture of Warwick society at the time. No wonder Mrs Simmonds bought the filthy old feathers, if feather beds were so expensive and it would appear that Mrs Willmot kept a superior inn or had a large family for she bought five pairs of sheets, the most expensive being 13sh. If 3 shillings represented half a week's wages for some people, some of the purchases can be seen to be extremely expensive by today's standards.

Other fascinating entries in the account books included

> One pound of candles − 5d
> Powdering tubb − 3sh
> Cullender − 6d
> 3 old sponges − 1sh
> 2 quire ordinary writing paper − 1sh
> 1 yd silver lace for shoes − 2sh 6d
> Pewter bed pan and 2 pair of hand irons − 3sh 6d

James Fish himself bought several items including two muslin neckcloths at 2sh, two old shirts at 5sh and a pair of shoes 8sh 6d. His wife bought a chamber pot and 2 basins 8d, a pair of scissors and old spectacles 8d and a pair of shoes 14sh, amongst other things. Mary Fish bought 5 pair of ruffles 2sh, 2 fans 1sh 6d, a pair of shoes 12sh and 2 mobbs for 3sh.

Some of my favourite entries included—The hospital man buying a little mash for 5d and a cooler for 3d (perhaps to brew beer?) and Mr Hopkinson paid 10sh 6d for pamphlets & waste paper! (Was recycling in progress, even in 1733?) Mr Paris (of the famous family of metal craftsmen in Warwick?) bought the silver hilted sword and old Caine for 12sh and Thomas Potter paid 8d for "one old and two young ducks new hatcht". The same man paid 3 guineas for "the cow but deducting 18 pence for the two cowkeepers and 3d spent".

The list of entries was rendered fascinating by James Fish, because the entries were so neat as to be easily readable and included so many details, as to fire the imagination. The more one analyzed the entries, the more interesting they became.

The Treasure.

It was small wonder that the octogenarian Ann Johnson had refused to part with the key to her treasure until shortly before her death, when the value of the gold and silver coins alone came to over £120! There were coins which previously I had only heard mentioned in connection with the treasure chests of Pirates—such coins as Lewis dores, Moydores and French Guineas. To think that a large collection of gold items lay in a chest, hidden in Landor House, was quite breathtaking! The coins were expertly weighed and sold accordingly, but many of the items of jewellery were valued after contact with a firm in Birmingham.

The contents of the treasure chest made exciting reading.

The diamond necklace – £14
One large silver salver – £8 2sh
One gold watch – £9 9sh
One other gold watch – £10
One gold chain for a watch – £3 3sh 10d
One gold necklace, 70 beads & 3 odd beads – £1 5sh 7d
Six gold rings – £2 19sh 7d
One mourning ring – 9sh 7d
Four pairs of gold buttons – £1 9sh 9d
Two pairs of gold buttons – 15sh 9d
20 Scepter peeces, 2 half scepters and one quarter of a scepter peece by tale – £26 11sh
14 peeces of other gold (2oz 15dr 18g) – £10 11sh 10d
45 peeces of old silver coin – £2 10sh
10 gineas and 2 Lewis dores and an half – £12 11sh 3d
5 Moydores one French Ginea & one Lewisdore – £8 11sh 6d

There were numerous other items and when you consider the vast sums of money which the Johnsons had spent during their lifetime (including the hundreds of pounds on legal fees) it is made clear just how lucrative had been the career of the competent Doctor. Some of the items were not sold immediately and some of the jewellery was eventually sold for less than the valuation, but this did not detract from the vast quantity of precious items, collected in an age before reliable banks were available.

£2,424 Raised By Sales of Property

Where Ann Johnson and James Wright had failed, the persistent James Fish succeeded and in 1734, the Irish Estates were sold to the Irish Agent for approximately their true value. James Fish, backed by the other Trustees, demanded the Irish accounts for the past 30 years and thus quelled any attempt to defraud the charity. The Irish estates realised £1,300 and over £1,000 was raised by the sales of the contents of Landor House.

Much of the furniture and fittings of Landor House were purchased by the first tenant of the property Thomas Archer, who paid the Charity Trustees £125 in December 1734.

In 1735, the Trustees decided to buy Hogbrook Farm near Tachbrook, so that the Charity would have a steady income from the rent, whilst still retaining the security of land ownership. However, as usual in any transactions connected with the Johnsons, there were many complications and in 1737, yet another Chancery Decree had to be obtained, after yet another law suit! This time, James Wright presented a bill of £65 8sh 5d, so he was still finding the work lucrative!

Interestingly, the Charity experienced temporary cash-flow problems and Francis Smith, presumably the richest of the Trustees, lent £200 to make up the extra money needed for the purchase of the farm.

During 1734, James Fish claimed £26 from the Charity, plus another £25 for making out the many lists. However, this money seemed to be just payment for the innumerable hours of work put in by the diligent Chief Trustee and in after years, when the Charity affairs went smoothly, it was largely thanks to the huge efforts of James Fish.

From March 1733, for around eighteen months, James Fish was working at Landor House almost every day doing the enormous task of sorting, listing and selling and later he frequently travelled to Hogbrook Farm. I like to think of the busy 61 year old, galloping off on his horse down the Banbury Road to sort out yet another problem!

The Recipients of the Charity.

Not only did James Fish keep accurate accounts of money received, he also kept detailed records of how the money was spent. Mr Fish tended to hand out small amounts of money to a larger number of people and the accurate descriptions he took the trouble to write give us an insight into the social history of the period. However by giving reasons as to why money had been given, James Fish seemed to allow the poor people to keep their dignity. It is difficult to despise a person as being poor and inadequate if you know why they have fallen on hard times. For instance we feel only sympathy for the folk of Bridge End who were flooded out, or Thomas Sharpe who fell from his horse.

The following is a selection from the vast number of entries which James Fish wrote between the years 1733 – 39.

Gave Mr Roe being sick and weak – 2sh
Gave Richd Rawlins being lame – 2sh
Gave blind Mrs Gardner – 5sh
Gave Goody Post 2sh & Parsons the School Mistress 2sh
Gave old Barnicle to bury his wife – 5sh
Gave the poor in bridge end after the great flood
  (Sept. 10th 1735) – 3sh
Gave Thomas Sharpe bad with a fall from his horse – 2sh
Gave Goody Woodcock lying in – 1sh
Gave Ffells girle at her going to service – 4sh
Gave old Widow Bench long bedridden – 2sh 6d
Gave Heycocks chd sick with measells – 2sh
Gave Coles poor wife a week in labour – 2sh
Pd Wid Yeborn towards placing out her girl – £2 10sh
Gave Goody Woodcock with a sore brest – 6d
Sent Widow Blason by Nurse Burch – 1sh
Gave Wm Perkins wife long under the chiurgons hands – 2sh 6d
Gave Thomas Williams for to buy a shirt – 4sh
Gave blind Charles Smith – 5sh

Widows figured prominently in the lists, often being given only 6d or a shilling. However it was probably fairer to try to spread the money to as many recipients as possible.

James Fish would have known most of the poor people personally, certainly all those in St Mary's parish. With a father who had been Parish Clerk for 20 years and himself Church Warden in 1730 – 1, James would have familiar with the life history of almost every inhabitant.

The poor of the Parish of St Nicholas he might not have known so well, but with a population of only 3,000 to 4,000, the town of Warwick was still small enough to be a fairly tight community.

The important thing was that James Fish seemed to care about the needs of those less fortunate than himself and I like to imagine various poor people being overjoyed with an unexpected gift of a shilling. I think James would have enjoyed playing 'The Bountiful Uncle' to the deserving poor without making them feel uncomfortable.

Thomas Archer M.P. Accuses Warwick Corporation of Corruption.

After many of the household goods had been sold and repairs had been carried out, Thomas Archer took out a 21 year lease on Landor House, commencing in December 1734.

Being a member of the well known Archer family, whose ancestral home was at Umberslade, near Tanworth, Thomas probably knew Warwick well, as the family had a town house in Jury Street. Although the name Thomas was common to several generations in the early eighteenth century, almost certainly the Thomas Archer renting Landor House was the man who became Whig M.P. for Warwick in the 1734 election.

Born in 1695, in Knowle, Thomas and his brother Henry were elected in peculiar circumstances. In those days, it was usual for the Earl of Warwick to nominate the two members of Parliament and elections were a mere formality.

However for some years during the early part of the eighteenth century, the reform-seeking Whig party had been trying to secure the seats without success. Bribery was common and many stories abounded. The Castle nominees were usually Tory and so was the Mayor. In 1734, the Whigs petitioned and although the Tory Mayor increased the number of men eligible to vote from around 700 to 1,007, the Tory nominees were defeated and the Whigs Thomas and Henry Archer were elected.

So from the outset the Archer brothers were unpopular with the Mayor and Corporation, who must have an inkling of what was to come. In 1737, Thomas Archer, Henry Wise and the churchwardens of St Nicholas began a Chancery Suit. The Mayor and Corporation were accused of corruption concerning the mismanagement of the town's finances!

There should have been sufficient money from the King Henry VIII Estate to pay for whatever was needed in Warwick, but too much had been spent on feasting. The new Court House, which had cost £2,250 had been partly financed by borrowed money.

The outcome of the Chancery Suit was that the Corporation was deemed to be guilty, if only in part and in 1739, the town finances were placed under the control of Chancery. A debt of £4,000 had to be repaid and not until 1769 did Warwick Corporation have the right to control the town's finances again.

Thomas Archer must have been extremely unpopular with some in Warwick! At the period when the Chancery Suit was being prepared, Landor House must have been the venue for numerous meetings between the Member of Parliament, the Churchwardens of St Nicholas and perhaps the 84 year old Henry Wise, then living in the nearby Priory.

Whilst Thomas Archer was the tenant, there were various problems with repairs to the house and garden maintenance.

Generally James Fish dealt with Mr Archer's agent and in 1738, a letter was sent by the Chief Trustee complaining about, "Great abuse done daily at Mr Archer's garden." Could it have been that eighteenth century vandals were at work because Thomas Archer had upset so many in the town?

In 1741, not surprisingly, Thomas Archer was unseated and became M.P. for Bamber instead, although his brother Henry continued to represent Warwick. In 1741, Thomas inherited the family estate at Umberslade and in July 1747, he was created a peer, becoming Lord Archer, Baron of Umberslade. Thomas Archer had the Nuthurst Obelisk erected near Tanworth, to celebrate his elevation to the peerage and after his death at Pirgo in Essex in 1768, he was buried in the church at Tanworth.

Repairs to Landor House. Bricks 2 Shillings Per 100!

During the early years of the tenancy of Thomas Archer, many repairs were carried out at Landor House. In 1733, the first repairs were carried out by John Townlin, on the orders of Francis Smith, the famous builder, acting in his position as Trustee.

Later in 1737, extensive repairs were carried out by William Tatnall and his workmen. For "six days work of myself" William Tatnall charged 9 shillings, but other less skilled workmen were paid only 1 shilling a day or sometimes 1sh 3d. It seemed that William Tatnall did the bricklaying himself and the price of the bricks was 2 shillings per 100.

In 1735 many carpentry repairs had been carried out, by Ed. Williams and new rafters had been fitted to most of the outbuildings, such as the barn, the stables, the leanto and the coach house. It is difficult to picture the site of the present playground, when the greenhouse had new door cheeks and the stables had a new manger!

One tiny piece of much folded paper interested me very much. On it were written in pencil many extremely complicated long division sums. Apparently they were the calculations of the wood needed to complete Mr Archer's parlour wainscot. I marvelled at the numerical competence of the worker (the sums were correct, I checked on my calculator!) and I could imagine the scrap of paper being carried about in a pocket for several days.

The Cottages (Coach and Horses)

It was fortunate for workmen repairing Landor House that the adjoining building was an inn! James Fish itemised many payments for the "Workmen's allowance for drink." On March 17th 1734, a bill for 12sh 4d was paid and I imagine quite a quantity of ale could have been bought for that amount. In the eighteenth century it seemed that it was considered necessary to treat the workmen well, if you wanted a good job doing.

Repair work was done to the 'Coach and Horses' also. In 1738 William Tatnall charged 6sh 9d for

"4 days and half more of myself about repairing & white washing the two houses & tiling the pigsty & making up a wall between the muckel hole and the stable."

That extract describing the present yard between the cottage and Eastgate conjures up a wonderful picture!

The Death of Francis Smith 1738.

The first of the Trustees to die was Francis Smith at the age of 66. He was only a year older than James Fish and the two men had known each other for many years. Having lived and had his business premises at the Marble House, Francis Smith was a famous and much mourned citizen of Warwick.

As there were supposed to be at least three trustees of the charity, William Smith took over the position from his father and James Fish seemed to have much respect for him also.

The Death of James Fish 1740

By March 1740, James Fish was very ill and he died in May at the age of 67. He was buried on 11th May at St Mary's Church.

The career of James Fish had been a long one, the numerous surveys of the Warwick area being made from 1686, until shortly before his death. Many of his maps, now housed in Warwick County Record Office are a sheer delight to examine, with appealing paintings adorning some and all being labelled with the same, ultra-neat, legible writing. Meticulous, even with account books, one glance at the neatly ruled columns and clear, well formed writing told you that here was a talented man, proud of his own high standards.

All the maps and surveys he was concerned with seemed to be in areas within easy travelling distance from Warwick. Wasperton, Kenilworth, Tachbrook, Hampton Lucy, Knowle and many others could all have been reached daily and I wondered if James had some aversion to spending nights away from his home in Church Street. Perhaps losing his books and mathematical instruments when the family home was destroyed in the fire of 1694, had made him extra wary.

Fine surveyor as he was, I believe that the charity bearing Ann Johnson's name was perhaps his finest contribution to the history of Warwick. It may have been Ann Johnson's property and money, but it was James Fish who organised the Charity from drawing up the rough plans of the Trust Deed to setting the daily organization on a sure footing. The enormous efforts put in by James from 1733 to 1739 must have made the Charity hundreds of pounds of extra money and whilst reading the copious memoranda he wrote, I sensed he was proud to be granted the opportunity to organize something so important for posterity.

Since his time, many generations of poor and needy people in Warwick have been helped as a result of his devotion to duty, and the fact that the Charity developed into one of the most important in Warwick is largely due to his influence.

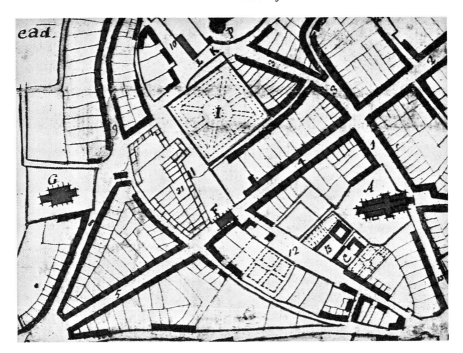

THIS MAP OF WARWICK IN 1711 WAS DRAWN BY JAMES FISH THE YOUNGER.
Beautifully clear, the map is unusual in that North is shown at the bottom, not the top. Being one of the maps included in the set "The Town Maps of Warwick 1610–1851" prepared by the County Record Office and published by the Museum, it provides a fascinating picture of Warwick less than twenty years after Landor House was built. It is interesting to note that the site of Landor House and the cottages is still shown occupied by 6 separate dwellings, 4 fronting Smith Street and 2 in Chapel Street.
St Mary's Church is labelled A, The College B, The Deanery C, Eastgate F and St Nicholas' Church G. The large square labelled I is a Vineyard Garden in the Castle Grounds. (W.C.R.O.)

The very existence of Landor House today perhaps owes more to James Fish than anyone else as had he not helped Ann Johnson achieve her ambition, after her death the house might have been taken by the lawyer in lieu of payments. In private hands, when the house fell into disrepair, as it did on several occasions, various sections might have been demolished and the entire site might have had a vastly different history.

The will of James Fish was a carefully constructed affair, leaving his several small properties to his wife Hannah and sister Mary. Apparently having no other immediate family, legacies were left to various cousins. I laughed when I read that James had left sister Mary "the feather bed and bedstead" as songs mentioning this occurrence had always amused me! Dr Bree was left one guinea to buy him a ring and to thank him for "his great kindness to me and my family."

It was interesting to note that the will had been drawn up by lawyer Richard Wright (perhaps the son of James?) Less than 40 years later, Richard Wright's grandaughter was to move into Landor House, with her father Dr Walter Landor.

Dr Bree.

After the death of James Fish, I must admit the research became somewhat more difficult and far duller. No one else bothered to write about the everyday occurrences at Landor House or the Charity business in such detail.

Doctor Bree (perhaps Dr Johnson's successor in the medical practice) took over the writing of the accounts, as the only remaining original Trustee. The entries of money given to the poor seemed to take on a medical flavour, for example,

> July 30th 1743 Gave to Mrs Ingram (being lunatick) for defraying the expense of sending her to London to get her into Bedlam hospital − £2 12sh 6d
> Feb. 10th 1743/4 Gave Harper being disordered in his senses − £2 2sh

Being a conscientious Trustee, he was a regular visitor to Landor House, whenever any problems arose, but he was clearly not as obsessed with the Charity business as had been James Fish.

Thomas Bree died around 1752 and William Smith continued as Trustee till his death in 1747. From then on, the Trustees became more in number (often six or more) and the names included many prominent men of Warwick.

Various Tenants.

One of the benefits of Landor House and the cottages being let for Charity was that from the charity accounts, we find the names of all the tenants over the centuries.

After Thomas Archer's lease had expired, various others rented Landor House. In 1753, Charles Shuckborough, a physician, was in residence (presumably the same person who later became a Baronet and Charity Trustee).

In 1757, Mr Beardesley was paying a slightly reduced rent of £20 and he continued his occupation till 1770.

The Cottages.

Until 1768, the cottages were still known as "The Coach and Horses" and the inn continued to flourish. After Thomas Bolton, the premises were leased to Mr Dixon, Thomas Taylor and later Mrs Taylor, for an annual rent of £8 10sh.

Apparently, in Warwick during the eighteenth century, there had been a large number of inns. During the latter part of the century, many were converted back to private houses and so it was with the cottages. As there were in reality two houses, for the first time for nearly two centuries the cottages were leased separately, probably bringing in more money for the Charity as a result.

The larger cottage nearest Eastgate, still had a large yard and so continued to be let as business premises. The Salloway family, who were carpenters, rented the property for many years, together with a small garden. The smaller cottage was rented by the Robinson family, likewise through several generations. In those times, life must have been stable, if perhaps boring by our standards, with numerous people living their entire lives in the same house.

THE LANDOR FAMILY

Above the impressive front door of Landor House there is a sign proclaiming vaguely, "Landor Born 1775." This refers to the famous writer Walter Savage Landor, but today few people know that.

In the days when Walter Savage Landor and his family lived in the house, the official name was Eastgate House. The renaming of the property 'Landor House' only took place a century ago, in November 1892.

The sign above the front door was placed in position on January 30th 1888, nearly twenty four years after the death of the writer. That January day in 1888 was

MEMORIALS TO WALTER SAVAGE LANDOR.

The impressive front door of Landor House with "Landor Born 1775" written above.

The Landor Memorial in St Mary's Church, Warwick, unveiled on Jan. 30th 1888 – the 113th anniversary of Walter Savage Landor's birth.

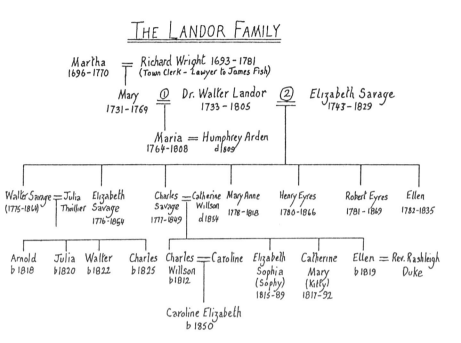

the 113th anniversary of Walter Savage Landor's birth and it was chosen as an appropriate date to unveil a bust of the writer in St Mary's Church. Set in a niche on the reverse of one of the main pillars in the Nave, the bust is still much admired.

At the unveiling of the bust in 1888, a gathering of notable people included The Mayor Alderman Stanton, The Countess of Warwick, Miss Ryland, Miss Percy and Alderman Kemp (the local historian) along with representatives of the Landor, Southey and Kingsley families. Walter Savage Landor had been friendly with many literary figures of his day, which explained the interest of the Southey and Kingsley families. Possibly, after the ceremony in St Mary's Church, some, if not all of the dignitaries, adjourned to Landor House for a small ceremony as the plaque was unveiled.

Whilst it would now seem reasonable that the house is named after him, Walter Savage Landor did not spend as much time in Warwick as other members of his family, some of whom lived in Landor House all their lives.

Doctor Walter Landor.

Dr Walter Landor, the writer's father, was the first member of the family to have any connection with Landor House.

Doctor Landor moved to Warwick in 1760, after completing his medical degree. Although he was heir to a considerable estate in Staffordshire, he determined to practise medicine until his inheritance materialized. He married Mary Wright, daughter of Richard Wright (later to become Town Clerk of Warwick) and it is believed that the newly weds lived in a house in Sheep (now Northgate) Street. Wherever the young Landors were living, their lives were not particularly happy as during the next nine years, four of the five daughters born to the couple died in infancy. Only Maria, born in 1764, survived and it must have been particularly galling for a well qualified Doctor to experience so many deaths in his own family.

During this period, Dr Landor, as a respected resident of the town, became one of the Trustees of Ann Johnson's Charity. As such, he would have been aware of the potential of Landor House to become perhaps the best situated private house in Warwick.

In 1769, Dr Landor suffered yet another blow when his wife herself died, at the age of only 38. She was buried in St Mary's Church and the memorial tablet to Mary Landor and the four infant daughters can still be seen near the north wall in the Regimental Chapel.

In 1774, Dr Walter, then a 41 year old widower, with a 10 year old daughter, decided to marry again and this time his bride was a local heiress Elizabeth Savage of Bishops Tachbrook. Other branches of the Savage family owned estates in various parts of Warwickshire (some of which were eventually inherited by Dr Walter Landor) and it was said that on her marriage, 30 year old Elizabeth brought with her annuities of over £4,500.

So around 1774 (Dr Walter was then Secretary for Ann Johnson's Charity and the account books are missing) the wealthy, yet hardworking couple moved into Landor House. Dr Landor continued his medical practice for the next 20 years and Elizabeth bore 7 healthy children during the next nine years.

The Landor Children. Frequent Arguments.

Dr Walter and Elizabeth Landor must have been overjoyed as their family grew. Walter, Elizabeth, Charles, Mary Ann, Henry, Robert and Ellen arrived almost in successive years. It is interesting to note whilst the three eldest children were given the second name of Savage, after their mother's maiden name, the youngest boys were given the name of Eyres, after their maternal grandmother who had been a member of the old Whitnash family of that name. In the late eighteenth century, it was important that old family connections were recognized.

In the early years of the Landor family's occupation, Landor House must have been overflowing, large though it was. Visitors and dinner parties were common and there were generally five resident servants, besides the growing family.

In some ways, the household seems to have been rather undisciplined, with both parents famous for losing their temper. Walter the eldest son seemed to have inherited a bad temper and he was frequently rude to his parents and guests.

A delightful anecdote was related years afterwards by the writer Mary Sherwood, who as a small child had visited the Landors with her mother in 1782.

> "When we arrived at the Doctor's house, we were ushered into a parlour, where Mrs Larnder received us very cordially; but before the fire, for there were fires all that summer, lay her eldest boy Walter, a big boy with rough hair. He was stretched on the carpet and on his mother admonishing him to get up, he answered 'I won't' or 'I shan't.' She reproved him and he bade her hold her tongue."

This story seems to illustrate the universal problem of defiant children! Walter was perhaps following in the footsteps of the "undutiful" Henry Johnson—it was fortunate that the Landors were a united and forgiving family on the whole.

Elizabeth, who was about the same age as the visitor was more hospitable. She took Mary Sherwood upstairs to her playroom (presumably one of the garrets?) and showed off her dolls, saying,

> "I am glad you came today, for you have saved me from a good scolding, my mother is so much out of humour."

Mary Sherwood went on to give a delightful picture of Dr Landor and his wife.

> "And in truth the poor lady, though exceedingly civil and hospitable, was in such a perpetual fume, that her husband, a hearty, old-fashioned sort of man, a physician of the by-gone days, kept constantly saying to her at dinner, 'Come Betty, Keep your temper; do Betty, keep your temper.' "

These vivid sketches of Landor life are included in several biographies of the eldest son Walter.

Dr Landor—an Influential Figure.

As an outspoken, educated person, Dr Landor was much concerned with local politics. An ardent Whig supporter (until the horrors of the French Revolution made him change his views and cross with Edmund Burke to the Tory side) he helped to break the Earl of Warwick's influence on the selection of Members of Parliament. In 1774, Dr Landor led an Independent Party which forced an election to be held (the first since 1734 when the Archers had been elected.) Normally the Earl's two nominees, in this case two of his brothers, were returned unopposed. However Dr Landor and his followers succeeded in securing the election of Robert Ladbroke, a city banker with an estate at Idlicote, for one of the Parliamentary seats. This victory for Dr Landor and the Whigs must have angered the Earl greatly!

As might have been expected, before long Dr Landor became a J.P. The Quarter Sessions were held four times a year at the Shire Hall and a number of less serious crimes were tried including vagrancy, prostitution and disorderly conduct. The usual punishments meted out by Dr Landor and the other J.P.s were a public whipping through the main street of Warwick, from Westgate to Eastgate, or up to six months in gaol.

A Country Gentleman

In 1781, Dr Landor inherited the Rugeley Estate in Staffordshire from his father, together with other properties, which brought in a sizeable income each year. In 1786, Dr Landor had an unexpected slice of luck when he was left Ipsley Court, a house and estate eighteen miles west of Warwick, by John Norris, a second cousin of Mrs Landor. Also as the eldest of four daughters, Mrs Landor had a quarter share in the family estate at Tachbrook. At this period, it has been suggested that Dr Landor's income then exceeded £700 a year.

There can be little doubt that the Landors were high on the social ladder and lived as members of the landed gentry were expected to live. After he finally retired from his medical practice in 1794, Dr Landor divided his time between his estates, following the pursuits of a typical English gentleman. At this time, when the family were in residence, Landor House must have been one of the social centres of Warwick. The best of furniture, food, wine, clothes and household items were to be found there. On the whole, the Landors were good organisers and enjoyed their money and privilege. Apparently the servants were well treated and appreciated working in the "Finest house in Warwick", which was how the Landor family seemed to refer to their rented home.

In retrospect, perhaps this period was the most glorious in the long history of the old house. In 1788, the wedding of 24 year old Maria must have been one of the social events of the year and Landor House on that day must have been a hive of genteel activity! From her grandfather Richard Wright (who had died in 1781 at the age of 88) Maria had inherited £11,000 apart from a considerable amount of property. Her marriage to Humphrey Arden (a distant cousin and a member of the old Warwickshire family well known because of the connection with Shakespeare's mother) would have been considered a suitable one for someone in her position. In those times, arranged marriages between suitably well endowed partners were still considered desirable and Maria was the only one of Dr Landor's daughters to marry and leave Landor House. The others spent almost their entire lives in the house.

Sadly money did not bring happiness to Maria, who died unexpectedly in 1808 only 3 years after her father. Having nursed her invalid husband for several years in that town, Maria was buried in St James' Church in Bath, her husband following her to the grave a year later.

In 1805, Dr Landor died of cancer aged 72, presumably whilst at home in Landor House. By all accounts, his was a long and lingering death and until the end on November 3rd Landor House must have been rather a sad place.

Despite many advantages, life had not been easy for Dr Walter. True, he had enjoyed his short retirement, but attacks of gout had sometimes curtailed activities. Probably after the traumas of his first marriage, his greatest disappointment was his eldest son Walter, who, having no head whatsoever for business, lost money at an alarming rate. Both men possessing a bad temper, it was small wonder that their quarrels were many. However, young Walter was reconciled with his father at the last and wrote the Latin inscription for his father's memorial in Bishops Tachbrook Church, which proclaimed his father to have been,

"Pleasant, learned, liberal, upright, most delightful to his friends."

Dr Samuel Parr.

During the last fifteen years or so of Dr Landor's life there were frequent visits being made to Landor House by two extremely interesting characters. Both men were famous for different reasons and since they were friendly with each other, it is more than likely that they visited together.

Dr Parr was a noted classical scholar, who since 1783 had been Curate of Hatton, about three miles from Warwick. He was a strong Whig and his brick parsonage, with its excellent library, became a meeting place for the learned, the literary and the eccentric.

Young Walter Savage Landor was very friendly with Dr Parr and the two men seemed to respect each other. It is said that Dr Parr once left his own dinner guests at Hatton to ride to Landor House to visit young Walter, just returned to Warwick. The two used to walk or ride to Leamington (along what is now the Myton Road) before the place became large or fashionable.

Besides having a brilliant mind and being a witty conversationalist, the pipe smoking, bell-ringing devotee was considered eccentric. He was often seen on the road between Hatton and Warwick, dressed very oddly in an old blue cloak and an enormous cauliflower-like wig. With a slight lisp and pompous way of talking, Dr Parr was not easy to ignore.

He had been born in Harrow in 1747 and had taught at Harrow School for a time. After studying at Cambridge and taking Holy Orders in 1769, he had had various posts in schools and churches, until he settled in Hatton. That village must have been a lively place during Dr Parr's residence as scholars from far afield, including Lord Byron and Lord Lytton the novelist, travelled to make his acquaintance.

During his lifetime, he wrote many books and in 1820 actively defended Queen Caroline when there was a public scandal and her name was ordered to be omitted from official prayers. Often nicknamed "The Whig Dr Johnson" Dr Parr was once reputed to have met that other worthy scholar and the outcome was that neither would give an inch in the witty conversation.

When Dr Parr died in 1825, the world lost a great and kindly man. He was buried in the church at Hatton, deeply mourned by many, especially the poor.

I wonder what Mrs Landor in particular, thought of Dr Parr? I expect both she and Dr Landor secretly admired much he did, but tut-tutted at some of his eccentricities!

Dr William Lambe. Early Vegetarian.

Dr Lambe visited Landor House frequently from 1794 to 1805, because he took over Dr Walter Landor's medical practice on his retirement. Both Dr Lambe and

Engraved by H. Meyer

THE REV? SAMUEL PARR, L.L.D.

From 1783 until the time of his death in 1825, this famous and learned man was Curate of Hatton near Warwick. Keenly interested in politics, he was often nicknamed "The Whig Dr Johnson". An eccentric, yet kindly character, Dr Parr was a particular friend of Walter Savage Landor. Today although one of the wards at the Central Hospital, Hatton is named after him, the name of Samuel Parr has become largely forgotten. (W.C.R.O.)

his wife Harriet were great friends of Walter Savage Landor and sometimes Dr Lambe and the writer would visit Dr Parr together.

Born in Hereford in 1765, Dr Lambe was educated at Hereford Grammar School and St John's College, Cambridge. He had been attracted to Leamington by hearing of the saline springs from Benjamin Satchwell, who had travelled around, trying to interest doctors in its properties. Perhaps because of his own fragile health, Doctor Lambe was interested and he conducted experiments, publishing an 'Analysis of Leamington Spa Water' in 1794.

An early believer in a vegetarian diet, Dr Lambe ate only vegetables and fruit, drinking small quantities of distilled water and nothing else. He made a special study of cancer and sometimes asked his patients to follow a diet.

Around 1805, Dr Lambe left Warwick for a practice in London, but soon his wife and youngest child died from scarlet fever and when he read about this in the newspapers, Walter Savage Landor was extremely upset and wrote a poem "On the Dead" which was dedicated to Mrs Lambe.

Later in life, Dr Lambe became a Senior Fellow of the Royal College of Physicians and he treated the poets Keats and Shelley.

William Lambe died in 1847, aged 82, having been active until a year or so of his death. However, although he did not spend much over ten years in Warwick, I expect most of his patients would vividly remember the Doctor who ate raw potato, sliced in olive oil, as a salad for his breakfast!

In Warwick Library, there is a delightful book about Dr Lambe by H. Saxe Wyndham, published in 1940 by the London Vegetarian Society for 6d. It is so tiny, it is easily overlooked.

Mrs Elizabeth Savage Landor

Elizabeth Savage, besides being a desirable heiress, must have been a woman of considerable character. It may have been a delightful change to leave her quiet, rural home in Bishops Tachbrook with its wonderful garden and open views, to live in the bustling County Town, as the wife of a successful doctor. However, with the speedy arrival of so many children, life must have been hectic.

By all accounts, Elizabeth had a formidable temper; in fact some biographers of her eldest son suggest that by her own lack of control, she encouraged him to be defiant. An amusing story concerning mother and son was related in several biographies. Home to Landor House for a vacation from school, Walter was speaking arrogantly and disrespectfully about the Archbishop of Canterbury, when company was present. Whereupon Mrs Landor rushed over, boxed Walter's ears and walked quickly away, her high-heeled shoes tapping on the polished floor as she went. The others present feared Walter might retaliate, but he merely shouted after her, "I'd advise you mother not to try that sort of thing again." Landor House must have been a lively place in those days!

After her husband died, Mrs Savage Landor proved a shrewd administrator of business affairs. She was very capable and possessed a great sense of justice. Unlike

WALTER SAVAGE LANDOR AGED 53.

This is a copy of a bust by John Gibson. Two copies were made and this is believed to be the copy given to Charles Dickens. This bust is now on exhibition near a doorway in the Romantics Room of the Regency Section of the National Portrait Gallery. The second copy was sent by Walter to his mother in Warwick. A similar bust stands above a doorway in Landor Hall today.

National Portrait Gallery.

her husband, she understood her eldest son's hatred of business and did her best to help him set his estates in order.

When Walter went to live abroad, he corresponded regularly, but the fact that he did not visit her in Warwick for the last fifteen years of her life saddened her greatly.

"A typical woman of her time" is how she has been described, but as her situation demanded, great emphasis was placed on duty. She loved Landor House, with its beautiful garden and she often entertained her sons and other members of the family.

Elizabeth Landor died in October 1829, only a few weeks short of her 86th birthday. Typically, she had been active and alert to within a short time of her death, having been engaged in her usual round of summer visits. Like her husband, parents and many of her ancestors, she was buried in St Chad's Church at Bishops Tachbrook and her memorial proclaimed,

"Elizabeth, daughter of Charles Savage, a most pious and excellent woman, wife and mother, living 85 years 11 months."

The Daughters of Dr Landor's Second Marriage.

Daughters Elizabeth born in 1776, Mary Ann born in 1778 and Ellen born in 1782 lived all their lives in Landor House, apart from visits to other family properties and various friends. Their mother instilled in them the importance of doing their duty and behaving as ladies of their class ought. If the girls ever did form any romantic associations, nothing came of them and all three girls remained unmarried. At that time, it was traditional for unmarried daughters to remain at home, as companions for their parents in their old age. Two of their four brothers also remained unmarried, but of course the boys went away to boarding school and university, before embarking on a career.

Mary Anne died in 1818 aged 40, over ten years before her mother, but Elizabeth and Ellen lived on for many years.

Elizabeth in particular was a very capable person, possessing many of the finer qualities of her parents and brothers. After the death of Mrs Landor, Elizabeth took control of the house, probably enjoying the extra responsibility. She was an excellent organiser, but perhaps inclined to be rather bossy towards Ellen.

In 1834, Elizabeth and Ellen started an Infant School at the lower end of Smith Street, not far from Landor House. At that time, education was becoming increasingly important and assisting a school would have been seen as a suitable interest for unmarried ladies of private means.

Perhaps it indicated Elizabeth Landor's frustration, but towards the end of her life, she took to calling herself Mrs E.S. Landor.

Ellen died in 1835 aged 53 and from then onwards unmarried nieces Sophy and Kitty frequently kept Elizabeth company in Landor House. By continuing to occupy the old family home, Elizabeth was helping to foster family unity and large family gatherings were common in the summer months.

ST NICHOLAS' INFANT SCHOOL IN SMITH STREET WAS FOUNDED BY ELIZABETH AND ELLEN LANDOR IN 1834. Ellen died the following year, but Elizabeth continued to take an interest until her death in 1854. The school finally closed in 1884, the premises being sold and the remaining scholars transferred to the Board School at Coten End. It is said that the proceeds from the sale of the house were used to help erect St Nicholas' Church Parish Room and Sunday School. Today the premises at 45 Smith Street are occupied by the 'Warwick Vac Shop' but the distinctive triangular canopy still remains over the door. (W.C.R.O.)

Her brother Henry Eyres referred to Elizabeth as "That greatest Aristocrat of our family," and certainly she seemed to wield much family power.

Christmas 1841

In 1841, at brother Walter's suggestion, Elizabeth invited her four brothers to spend one more Christmas Day together in their old home. It was a romantic idea and Elizabeth readily agreed to host a large family party in Landor House. Walter in particular seemed to enjoy Christmas and the whole family seemed to have happy memories of Warwick in late December.

We know that Walter arrived by coach from Bath, where he was then settled and his reunion with his family must have resembled the Victorian scenes, which are so often depicted on our Christmas cards today.

On a grey December afternoon, the door of Landor House would have been flung open allowing Walter to enter the cosy hall, decorated with plenty of holly, especially along the mantelpiece. Walter sometimes remarked to friends how he remembered the holly decorations of his childhood and no doubt Elizabeth would have organised the traditional items. Bunches of other evergreens would be hung on the panelling, with the coal fire in the elegant grate stirred into flame. The candles in the sconces on the walls would throw a soft, rosy glow around the stone flagged room and Walter's cheeks, warmed after the chill of his journey, would have seemed even redder.

Being the proud possessor of an enormous, infectious laugh, I expect he was soon engaged in amusing anyone within earshot with an animated description of his journey, which was often full of adventure! When a boy, his bedroom had probably been the small panelled room next to the large bedroom on the corner of Chapel Street. Probably his sister would have arranged for him to occupy his old room again, to give him extra pleasure.

On Christmas Day itself, I expect a large dinner was cooked in the kitchen in the Chapel Street wing of the house. Maybe they had turkey, plum pudding and mince pies, as was common at that period. Perhaps the Landors exchanged small home-made gifts as the wealthy often did and attended one of the Christmas services in St Nicholas' Church.

We know that Walter was extremely kind to those in need, especially at Christmas time, so perhaps the servants and former employees, such as his old nurse who still lived in Warwick, were given money.

Although the great Victorian revival of the Christmas festival was not yet underway, even without cards, Christmas trees and crackers, no doubt the Landors had a day filled with gaiety. After their Christmas dinner, perhaps the talk was of days long gone, when they were children together. Being a very united family, the Landors must have found that Christmas of 1841 a very emotional, but happy one, each brother relishing the visit to the home where he had been born over sixty years previously.

The Census Returns.

I have been very amused lately when various people ask what use census forms are, when the precise information is not released for 100 years. I dare say the forms are rather a chore, but to any social historian the information they contain is invaluable.

From the census returns of the mid nineteenth century, I discovered much about the inhabitants of Landor House, which could not have been obtained from the Account books of Ann Johnson's Charity.

From the Census Return of 1841, I learned of several other members of the Landor family, who were visitors to Landor House. The ageing Elizabeth not only had Mary, the 60 year old wife of brother Charles staying with her, but also Ellen Landor aged 20, Lucy aged 20 and Cecilia aged 15. To look after these five ladies,

CAROLINE ELIZABETH LANDOR IN 1863.
Caroline was the Great Niece of Walter Savage and Elizabeth Landor. At the time of the Census in 1851, she was living in Landor House, together with her mother and Great Aunt Elizabeth.
(W.C.R.O.)

there were five servants—Elizabeth Lydiatt aged 35, Mary Sue Yates 14, William Baker 30 and Nath Taylor 20. Presumably Elizabeth Lydiatt was the Housekeeper and William Baker the Butler.

In 1851, Elizabeth Landor had Caroline, the 32 year old wife of nephew Charles Willson, living with her. Also there was Caroline Elizabeth, aged one year, the daughter of Caroline and Charles. How Great Aunt Elizabeth must have enjoyed having the baby around. Also niece Sophy was living in Landor House, but unlike the others, was classed as a visitor.

The five Landors again had five servants to look after them. Lydia Thomas aged 41 was the cook, Thomas Hiron aged 31 was the butler and George Hancox 31, Emma Burton 24 and Frances ? (illegible) completed the list.

I found the information about Thomas Hiron particularly interesting. From the Account Books, I had learned that from 1852, when the property fell vacant, until her death in 1854, Elizabeth Landor had paid the rent of the adjoining cottage, so that a Thomas Hiron could live there. This puzzled me until I saw the census return. So kindly Elizabeth Landor paid £4 10 shillings a year rent, so that her Butler could live next door with his family. This same Thomas Hiron was presumably the servant who had been living in an outhouse of Eastgate when the 1841 census was taken.

The Garden of Landor House.

In the time of the Landors, the garden of the house was magnificent. Beautifully landscaped with sweeping lawns and majestic trees, including cedars, elms and at least one ilex, the garden was used as a place in which to stroll. Mrs Landor and daughters Mary Anne, Ellen and particularly Elizabeth, took a great interest and supervised activities.

In the years following the death of Mrs Landor, each summer there would be a large gathering of the family in the old house, Elizabeth enjoying being hostess. When staying at Landor House in the summer of 1839, Walter gave a delightful picture of the garden in a letter to a friend.

"Had you come to Warwick, I could have shown you the wood pigeons building and nightingales (or rather a nightingale) singing in my sister's garden, in spite of the eternal mowing and weeding."

In 1847, Sophy Landor wrote in her diary in July, "I was delighted to saunter up and down the large grass plot with Uncles Walter and Robert, hearing them discuss various writings."

Some idea of the size of the garden can be obtained from the map of Warwick in 1851. It would not be difficult to imagine Elizabeth, then aged 74, taking a leisurely walk round the trim borders or sitting for a while in the shade of one of the numerous trees.

When writing to a friend in 1852, Walter, then aged 77, mentioned having picked up from the gravel walk the first two mulberries that had fallen. He remembered

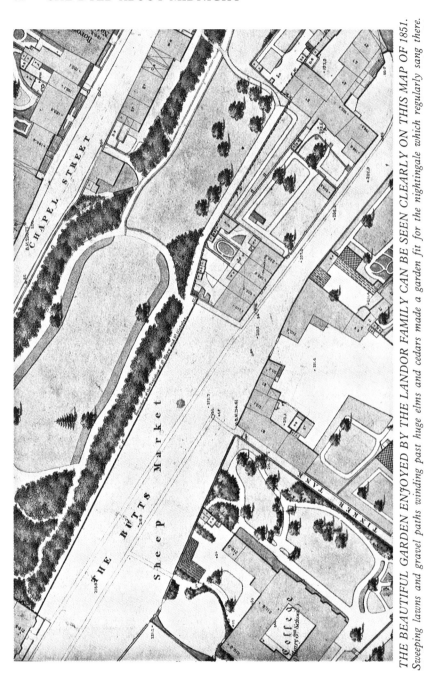

THE BEAUTIFUL GARDEN ENJOYED BY THE LANDOR FAMILY CAN BE SEEN CLEARLY ON THIS MAP OF 1851. Sweeping lawns and gravel paths winding past huge elms and cedars made a garden fit for the nightingale which regularly sang there. Unfortunately, the site was on the edge of three sections of the Warwick map and although Landor House is not shown, the extensive stable block, coach-house and Water House can be seen adjoining Chapel Street, to the right. (W.C.R.O.)

having done the same thing 74 years previously. There were few people as fortunate as the Landors—able to enjoy the same lovely garden throughout their entire lives.

The Death of Elizabeth

Walter visited his sister as usual in the summer of 1853, little realising that that would be his last visit.

In January 1854, Elizabeth suffered a stroke which caused paralysis. Niece Sophie nursed her until at 1 a.m. on February 24th, Elizabeth died.

Walter, then living in Bath, was unable to attend the funeral, but he was much affected by his sister's death. He told John Forster (a friend, later his biographer) that the loss of his earliest, dearest and nearly his last friend had deprived him of sleep, appetite, digestion, everything.

However about a month after Elizabeth's death, Walter was able to write a touching poem, describing the Warwick garden without his sister.

A Sister's Death.

Sharp crocus wakes the froward year;
In their old haunts birds reappear;
From yonder elm, yet black with rain,
The cushat looks deep down for grain
Thrown on the gravel walk; here comes
The redbreast to the sill for crumbs.
Fly off! fly off! I can not wait
To welcome ye, as she of late.
The earliest of my friends is gone.
Alas! almost my only one!
The few as dear, long wafted o'er,
Await me on a sunnier shore.

The Sons of Dr and Mrs Landor.

As might have been expected, all four sons grew up intelligent and well-educated young men. All four were sent away to excellent public Schools, the three eldest to Rugby but Robert the youngest to Bromsgrove Grammar School, which would have been slightly less expensive.

Wealthy as Dr Landor was, the family obviously spent much money maintaining their position in society and it was extremely costly educating four sons at the same time. So after Walter and Charles had proceeded to Oxford University, Dr Landor felt that one of the sons (probably Robert the youngest) was going to have to miss out University, on account of the cost. However Robert was extremely clever and passed a scholarship to Oxford, so that left the third son Henry Eyres, unable to attain a degree.

As so often happens, instead of ruining the chances of Henry, this disadvantage seemed to enhance them. Mrs Landor helped him with business deals and he became a Land Agent, after being articled to a firm of solicitors in London. Eventually Henry became the busiest and best respected Land Agent in the County. Henry Eyres is well remembered in the area today, in the form of roads named Landor Road (Whitnash and other places) and he endowed Whitnash School and aided other charities.

All the brothers continued to visit Warwick regularly, except for Walter who spent a number of years abroad. All of them seemed to have affection for Landor House, where they were born.

The brothers were long-lived, Walter dying at age 89, Charles at 72, Henry at 85 and Robert at 88 years.

Walter Savage Landor

Despite the fact that he still merits an entry in the "Dictionary of National Biography," there are many in Warwick today who know nothing of their famous poet, born in Smith Street. Although he travelled extensively abroad, Walter loved Warwick and returned frequently throughout his long life. Walter once wrote to the poet Southey,

"Never without a pang do I leave the house where I was born."

Early Life.

Born on 30th January 1775, Walter was the longed-for son and heir of Dr Landor. Within the previous decade, his father had lost his first wife and 4 daughters, so when his second wife Elizabeth gave birth to a son, within a year of their marriage, congratulations must have abounded. The day of young Walter's birth must have been one of the happiest ever in Landor House. A lover of good food and wine, Dr Landor probably drank a great many toasts that day.

To say that Walter was born with the proverbial silver spoon in his mouth, was perhaps an understatement! As Dr Landor's eldest son, he stood to inherit several estates and a considerable income, probably exceeding that of many other members of the Landed Gentry.

From an early age, Walter had to compete for his parents' attention with his numerous brothers and sisters, who arrived in successive years. When only 4 years of age, Walter was sent away to boarding school at Knowle, about 10 miles from Warwick, and from then on he only returned home in the school holidays. Perhaps this type of education, although much favoured at the time among the Middle and Upper Classes, was not the most sensible for a sensitive and intelligent boy, who seemed to need much love and praise.

At the age of eight, he was sent to Rugby School. When Walter excelled in some of his studies, notably writing Latin verse, what high hopes Dr Landor must have had for his eldest son. However long before he was due to leave for university, Walter was asked to leave the school because of indiscipline.

The problem seems to have been that he refused to obey orders unless he approved of them. When the Headmaster decreed that the sons of peers should be called 'Mister' Walter refused unless the rule was also applied to all the other boys. To many today it might appear that Walter possessed logical, forward thinking ideas, but in 1791, such ideas, coupled with a violent temper, inevitably led to conflict with the school authorities.

Not all were glad to see him leave however as Walter had been kind to his fags and claimed to be the first to pay a few pence a week to those unfortunate younger boys who did his chores. Also he had been kind to his younger brothers when they followed him to Rugby.

Although Walter might have been quite happy staying in Landor House for a while, exploring the contents of his father's library, well stocked with interesting travel books amongst the usual classics, it was decided that he should be sent to a private tutor in Derbyshire for a year or so. In 1793, Walter went to Trinity College, Oxford, but he lasted only a few terms before being rusticated, again for indiscipline. He had angered the authorities by being one of the first students to refuse to powder his hair, expressing Republican ideas and finally for firing a gun across a quadrangle in a fit of temper.

Following his return to Landor House, after spending some months in South Wales where he had a love affair and was said to have fathered a child, Walter had terrible rows with his father. In many ways the father, aged 61 and the son, aged 19 were alike in character and it is said that the rows were more about money than anything else. Walter resisted all attempts to settle him in a profession and around Christmas 1794, stormed out of Landor House, as he said—for ever. Walter had claimed his father had "used the most violent expressions" and on the face of it, few would blame him.

Fortunately after a year or so, Walter became reconciled with his father and once again spent lengthy periods at Landor House. Then interested in politics, he spent much time with Dr Parr, the Curate of Hatton, who was the adviser of many Whig politicians. Dr Parr, Dr Lambe and Walter were often together in Warwick and in December 1797, Walter accompanied Dr Parr to a mass meeting called to protest against Pitt's Budget proposals for an Income Tax, amongst other things. The meeting began in the Shire Hall, but had to adjourn to the Race-course, on account of the huge crowd which turned up. Those readers who dislike paying Income Tax today, may like to reflect that Walter and many other Warwick residents of the time did their best to prevent the tax being levied.

A Great Writer. Friend to Poets.

All his life Walter was a prolific writer and in 1798 his first long poem "Gebir" was published in Warwick by Henry Sharpe, as were the next two volumes of

A PENSIVE WALTER SAVAGE LANDOR AGED 64. First exhibited in 1840, this painting by William Fisher shows the famous poet in his favourite dark brown coat. As his popularity has waned in the twentieth century, this painting of Walter is now in store at the National Portrait Gallery in London.

National Portrait Gallery

poems. Southey, then a young critic, reviewed "Gebir" and Walter became well known in literary circles.

It is doubtful whether these volumes ever made any money, but in the 60 odd years which followed, Walter had many works of poetry and prose published. As he had been well versed in Latin, the rhythm of his construction frequently won him praise and later critics argued over whether his prose or poetry was the more memorable. Overall, however, he does not seem to have made any money from his writing, often having to resort to paying some of the publishing costs himself.

He became most famous for writing various volumes of "Imaginary Conversations" which brought him world wide acclaim. His company was frequently sought by other notable writers, who enjoyed his wit and brilliant conversation. Amongst others he met Charles Lamb, Wordsworth, Coleridge, Browning, Carlyle and Swinburne, but he became most friendly with the young Charles Dickens, who modelled the character of Mr Boythorne in "Bleak House" on him. Walter's long friendship with the Countess of Blessington, herself a well known literary figure, ensured his entry to many fashionable gatherings and his letters to her and other friends are a delight to read.

Perhaps Walter's main failing as a writer was that he refused to court popular taste, aiming his work at a select, well-educated audience. Therefore, much of his work is not readily understood today by modern readers unversed in the Classics. In 1850, when aged 75, Walter wrote in a letter,

> "I wrote chiefly to occupy the vacant hour, caring not a straw for popularity, and little more for fame."

A Lovable Character.

In 1811 impetuous Walter had married Julia Thuiller, a penniless girl of 17, who was 19 years his junior. Although the couple had four children, Arnold born in 1825, Julia in 1820, Walter in 1822 and Charles in 1825, they later separated amidst much bitterness. Walter was not interested in business and lost a large amount of money through unwise ventures, in particular buying an estate at Llanthony Abbey in Monmouthshire. In 1814 he and his wife were forced to flee abroad in order to escape creditors and for many years, they lived in Fiesole, near Florence. After the separation from his wife, who kept the villa in Fiesole, Walter lived frugally in England, settling the bulk of his income on his family, who seemed to have been reasonably comfortable.

At first I thought Walter Savage Landor was an arrogant waster, but I soon changed my mind. True he had a violent temper, but he was also a kind and generous person, with modern ideas of freedom and equality, years ahead of his time. He loved animals, especially dogs and treated them as if they were human. He owned a succession of dogs, but they did not travel to Warwick. Instead, when visiting Landor House, a dog named Oscar would accompany him on his numerous country walks. Walter loved flowers and trees in particular and thought gardens and the countryside in general were best left wild.

Unlike most of his contemporaries, Walter did not hunt. He even gave up shooting after he discovered a pheasant he had only wounded, dying in agony some hours later. He once had a tame marten and was very upset when it died.

A charming example of Walter's great attachment to trees was provided in a letter he wrote to Robert Southey in 1811. The subject was a privet bush which he had planted in the garden of Landor House.

> "I remember a little privet which I planted when I was about six years old and which I considered the next of kin to me after my mother and eldest sister. Whenever I returned from school or college—for the attachment was not stifled in that sink, I felt something like uneasiness until I had seen and measured it."

Visits To Landor House in Later Life.

After Walter had separated from his wife and settled in Bath in 1836, he visited Warwick almost every summer for a number of years. His sister Elizabeth would host a family gathering in Landor House and there were many amusing tales of his journeys.

In the summer of 1842, Walter arrived at Landor House by coach, but found that he had lost the key of his locked portmanteau. The following summer, he had remembered the key, but somehow had lost the portmanteau en route!

The summer of 1844 found Walter venturing on the train from London, but no-one told him that he had to alight at Coventry for Leamington. He sat tight and ended up in Birmingham, where he whiled away the time writing letters in a waiting-room, until the next train back. At that time, the railway station at Milverton had not been completed, so presumably, he had to finish his journey by coach.

I was much amused to read Walter's remarks concerning Leamington. In 1839, he wrote to a friend,

> "I wish he had brought you to Leamington instead of Malvern. But Malvern is the most healthy spot in the world, Leamington the most unhealthy... In fact the place is a sink."

Walter had been annoyed about the rise of Leamington in the Nineteenth Century—it made him angry that visitors had largely deserted Warwick for the newer town.

Walter Savage Landor was such a kind, talented yet unusual person, that many tales of his eccentricities are found. Not a lover of new clothes, his sisters Elizabeth and Ellen had to resort to strong measures when he visited the old family home. With his snuff coloured coat, crumpled linen and bulging boots, his sisters were often ashamed of his appearance. During the night, they would creep to Walter's room in Landor House and snaffle his old clothes, replacing them with new ones, which they hoped he would wear in the morning.

However although he rarely bought clothes, he was fastidious about cleanliness and was extremely fussy about what he ate and drank. Perhaps it was the influence of Dr Lambe, but Walter rarely drank much wine, often preferring water. His father and brothers all suffered from gout, but he did not and it was no surprise when he lived for longer than any of them. It was not unusual for Walter to buy and cook his own food, placing a high priority on good quality.

Last Visit To Warwick 1853. Walter Loses His Clothes!

The last visit which Walter ever made to the house in Smith Street sounded hilarious.

Once again he travelled by train, having to change at least once before reaching Landor House in the afternoon of August 15th. His niece Kitty was staying with his sister at Landor House, but when Walter arrived minus his luggage, the two unmarried ladies were posed with a problem. Walter had no night clothes and although there was a spare nightcap, male underclothes were unavailable in the house.

Walter was sure he had the bag and travelling box put on the train when he set out from Bath; in fact he had the keys to prove it, but somewhere along the route, he had lost both items of luggage. Walter was 78 years old and his sister 77 and the conversation in the Drawing Room of Landor House that afternoon must have been most amusing.

Messengers were sent out to the local railway stations, then even further afield to where he had changed trains, but no luggage could be found. Eventually, in the evening, a messenger had to be sent to Tachbrook, to borrow some clothes from brother Henry. After all this fuss and bother, I do not suppose Walter cared much about proper nightclothes but in polite society in Victorian times, such things mattered a great deal.

Eventually, a couple of days later, the luggage arrived quite safe and sound, so I expect Walter had a good laugh, as was his wont.

Sadly five years after his last visit to Warwick, Walter bowed to family pressure and in 1858, at the age of 83, went abroad to avoid scandal after a libel action against him. He had apparently been duped by a widow and her attractive daughter and he had later written a defamatory pamphlet about them. He fled to Florence, but his wife was unfriendly and only assistance from the poet Robert Browning helped the old man find suitable accommodation. Walter eventually died in 1864, mourned by only two of his sons and he was buried in the English Cemetry in Florence.

It was a lonely end for the colourful and talented character, after whom Landor House was named.

IN A QUIET CORNER OF THE VILLAGE CHURCHYARD AT BISHOPS TACHBROOK the wealthy bachelor Henry Eyres Landor and his two nieces were buried in the same grave, close to an old yew tree. Henry died in 1866 at the age of 86, Sophy in 1889 at the age of 74 and Kitty in 1892 at the age of 74. Henry's sisters, parents and numerous ancestors were buried inside St Chad's Church, which was close to the Savage's home. Henry's famous brother Walter, who was buried in Italy in 1864, has a memorial plaque inside the church.

Charles Savage Landor.

Born in 1777, Charles, like Walter was educated at Rugby School and later Oxford University. Only two years younger than his rebellious brother, when a boy Charles must often have been embarrassed by Walter's exploits.

Charles later became a clergyman and in 1806, he was appointed to the living of Colton, near Rugeley in Staffordshire, where he succeeded his uncle.

He married Catherine Willson, a distant cousin, and the couple had four children, including Mary Catherine, better known as Kitty and Elizabeth Sophia, better known as Sophy.

Charles and his family kept in close contact with the family in Warwick and frequently, the female members would stay for long periods in Landor House.

In 1849, Charles was the first of the four Landor brothers to die and his death was a shock to the entire family. He was buried at Colton, where he had spent 43 years as Rector.

Henry Eyres Landor.

Little did I think in my childhood days, as I scratched "Whitnash Endowed School" laboriously at the top of my papers with my cheap dip-in pen and brown watery ink, that it was Henry Eyres Landor I had to thank for the privilege. To my surprise, I found that Henry had indeed endowed a new village school in Whitnash in 1860.

Born in 1780, Henry followed his elder brothers to Rugby School, but as Dr Landor found he was not able to sustain the cost of keeping four sons simultaneously at university, Henry was afterwards sent to work in the office of a legal firm in London.

After some years, Henry returned to the Warwick area and soon became a highly respected and successful conveyancer. His keen business acumen enabled him to judge wisely and his advice was eagerly sought, not least by other members of the family.

In 1826, Mrs Landor helped Henry buy an estate in Whitnash which had once been connected with her family. He became Lord of the Manor and although the Manor House (demolished in 1962) continued to be leased to others, he took a great interest in the village.

Henry inherited a portion of his mother's Tachbrook estate and he purchased the remaining three quarters in 1832. Although maintaining his interest in Whitnash, he lived in 'Savage's House' at Tachbrook until his death in 1866. Seemingly rather shy, the wealthy bachelor was extremely kind to the villagers of Whitnash and Tachbrook and during his lifetime derived much pleasure from enlarging his mother's old home, with its delightful garden containing filbert and mulberry trees.

Robert Eyres Landor.

Like Walter, Robert Eyres merited a passage in 'The Dictionary of National Biography'. Robert too was a writer, although he was never as well known as his brother.

Born in 1781, the youngest of the four talented brothers, Robert went to Bromsgrove Grammar School, which was less expensive than the better known Rugby School. He was extremely clever and managed to pass a scholarship to Worcester College, Oxford, his father's old college. Dr Landor must have been delighted and it perhaps compensated the long-suffering father for the escapades of his rebellious eldest son.

In 1804, Robert was ordained and after some years of travel, he became Vicar of St Michael's at Hughenden in Buckinghamshire. The Norris family, who were relations of the Landors, were in possession of the estate and therefore the right to appoint the Vicar.

In those days of vested interest, posts were expected to be kept in the family and in 1824, Robert resigned in favour of a younger relative. For a time, Robert had

LANDOR HOUSE AS IT WAS IN THE TIME OF THE LANDORS.
The ground floor window to the right of the chimney in Chapel Street was later filled in, likewise the door to the right. Careful observation of the wall today reveals the site of the window. Some of the mature trees in the large garden can be seen behind the house. (W.C.R.O.)

acted as Chaplain in Ordinary to the Prince Regent, but he had not enjoyed this court post.

In 1829, his mother bought him the Living of Birlingham in South Worcestershire and there he remained for the rest of his life. He was a most conscientious parish priest and it was said that during his long years at Birlingham, he was never absent for a single Sunday. With an independent income, he could afford to be generous and sometimes gave away more than he received in stipend.

Throughout his life, Robert was a frequent visitor at Landor House, but often other members of the family would visit his sizable Rectory. He loved collecting pictures and when he died in 1869 at the age of 87, about fifty works including some by Rubens, Holbein, Raphael, Titian and Caraveggio were sold, along with his library of 1,600 books. Apart from a few personal bequests, all his assets were left to the church in Birlingham and over £4,000 was raised by the sale for the Restoration Fund.

ELIZABETH SOPHIA (SOPHY) LANDOR AROUND 1860. For many years till her Aunt Elizabeth's death in 1854, she stayed frequently at Landor House. Like many other unmarried daughters of her time, it fell to her lot to care for several older relatives. Sophy supervised the clearing out of Landor House in 1854 and she eventually inherited the Savage's family home in Tachbrook from her uncle Henry Eyres Landor. (W.C.R.O.)

Landor House in the Time of the Landors.

Throughout the 80 year occupation of Landor House by members of the Landor family, many improvements were carried out. The garden appeared to have been landscaped and generally outbuildings were tidied up.

As the house was aging, repairs were often necessary, but the family were often prepared to pay for some work themselves. In 1826, the Charity Commissioners reported that the house was old and frequently in need of repair.

The sash windows at the front of Landor House were probably put in in the early Nineteenth Century at the expense of the family. However these windows have come in for much criticism, not least from Alec Clifton Taylor in his book and television series, with the section on Warwick. Traditionalists argue that there should have been 12 panes not 8 for each window frame and maybe they are right.

Over the years, the rent paid by the Landors gradually increased. In 1800, only £30 per year was being paid, but by 1824, Mrs Landor was paying double that. In the last few years of Elizabeth's life, in the early eighteen fifties, the rent had increased to £75.

It always seemed odd to me that the Landor family paid out so much in rent over the years, especially when comfortable country estates had been inherited. I came to realise that the answer was that the Landor family loved their Warwick home and could not bear to leave. Certainly in the first part of the Nineteenth Century, Landor House, with its garden of around 1½ acres, was considered by many to be the finest house in Warwick.

1854. The End of the Landor Tenancy.

In the months following the death of Elizabeth Savage Landor, nieces Sophy and Kitty supervised the emptying of Landor House before the tenancy was terminated at the end of the year.

In her will, Elizabeth had left many items of furniture to specific members of the family. Sophy had "The little cabinet in The Drawing Room and the little cabinet in The Library." The family silver was distributed, with every family member having a share. Henry Eyres had the silver cream jug and Robert the four silver gravy spoons and sugar tongs. The list of silver items was long and it made one realise how magnificent the Landor possessions had been. The valuable items left by Ann Johnson had formed a long list, but the possessions of the wealthy Landors eclipsed that.

Elizabeth left money, mainly to the younger family members who were less wealthy. Sophy, Kitty and Walter's younger children were each left £2,000—a quite considerable sum in those times. In addition there were some shares, in particular some in the Stratford on Avon Canal Company which had once belonged to Dr Landor. Some of these shares were left for the benefit of the poor in Tachbrook, a kind inclusion in the best Ann Johnson tradition.

There were many paintings and whilst some were willed to family members, many of them were sold at auction in Warwick on 26th June. There was no auction in Landor House itself as Henry and his nieces felt they could not bear it.

"We could not endure the abomination of such a thing in the old House, nor the Garden to be trodden by the Rabble,"

Henry wrote to Walter later in 1854.

Poor Henry was left with a problem. He enquired of a relative,

"What can I do with the great Picture in the best Bed Room, a naked Venus?"

Walter had left this painting behind when he went abroad, but it was not to most Victorian tastes! Robert was pleased that the pictures he had selected and given to his sisters generally fetched more than those selected by Walter. It is interesting to think of the walls of Landor House covered by paintings which would be considered fantastically expensive today. In early Victorian times, the works of many old masters could be bought relatively cheaply.

Interestingly enough, when the rooms in Landor House were stripped, some of Walter's old manuscripts came to light. Also there were a number of copies of his earliest printed works.

EASTGATE IN THE EIGHTEENTH AND NINETEENTH CENTURIES

Charity Schools. Thomas Oken's Will

In the early eighteenth century, there was much interest in charity work in general and others in Warwick besides Ann Johnson left money for charitable purposes. A number of charities were set up to help the poor, but other citizens left money specifically for education, so that poor children could be helped to better themselves and hopefully stay out of trouble!

According to social history books, this movement towards charity schools was nationwide. In the London area alone, by 1712 there were 120 charity schools, but smaller towns like Warwick were also following the trend.

Since 1571, when Thomas Oken had left money for various charitable purposes, some money had been available for educating the poor children of Warwick. A wealthy merchant and past Guild Master, Thomas Oken had left £2 5 shillings annually towards augmenting the salary of the Master of the King's Grammar School, but a separate sum was also left to provide basic elementary education for the poor children. Oken gave "40sh. to the use of the schoolmaster to be found and kept in the town of Warwick for ever to teach petties and poor men's children within the said town."

Being keen on the preservation of old customs, Oken may have left this money to fund a substitute for an old choir school which had flourished for many generations previously near St Mary's Church, in The Butts. Mr E.G. Tibbits thought that in all probability, it was the remnant of the choir school which moved into St Peter's Chapel in 1700, under Master Thomas Meads. Certainly later records indicate that the money from Thomas Oken's Charity was paid to the Master of the Charity School, held in St Peter's Chapel, to pay for the education of 13 poor boys.

The Bablake School 1719.

If Thomas Oken's Charity provided the original funding for the Charity School, as seems likely, a couple of decades later other charities also became involved and the school became much larger.

The funding came from the wills of Mrs Sarah Greville in 1719, Earl Brooke in 1721 and Fulke Weale in 1729. Some charities supported children from St Mary's Parish and some supported children from the only other Parish of St Nicholas. Each of the charities was administered separately with a Trustee being appointed for each charity and Parish concerned to the Board of Trustees for the school. The Vicar and Churchwardens of each parish chose the pupils to be educated and the Board of Trustees appointed the schoolmaster. The master taught the boys, his wife taught the girls and living accommodation was provided for the couple and their family, on the upper floor of St Peter's Chapel.

To be offered a place at the Charity School must have been a marvellous opportunity for the poor youngsters, as not only was the schooling entirely free, but clothing was provided as well. According to the charity funding the free place, each pupil was clothed accordingly.

Most pupils were funded from Sarah Greville's Charity as 12 boys and 12 girls from each parish were educated and given all clothing, except shoes and stockings. The uniforms were blue and yellow and the Charity Foundation stipulated that once chosen by the Trustees, this clothing was to remain unchanged for all time. Small wonder that by the mid nineteenth century, these uniforms were considered very old fashioned!

Earl Brooke's Charity provided for 12 girls from St Nicholas' Parish. The colour of the uniforms was grey and gowns, petticoats, caps and tippets were provided.

The 13 boys who were funded by Oken's Charity were supplied with a coat and a pair of stockings annually. The coats were similar in design to those worn by the Beefeaters.

Some ten years after the establishment of the enlarged charity school, Fulke Weale (a woollen draper) left provision in his will for 2 boys to attend the school and also money for a clock and turret to be placed on St Peter's Chapel. At one time, Fulke Weale had been the representative for St Mary's Parish for Mrs Greville's Charity on the Board of Trustees and no doubt this had encouraged his interest in the school. The pupils funded by Fulke Weale's Charity were supposed to receive clothing, but sometimes they did not owing to lack of funds.

Funding.

The income from the charities involved came mainly from the rents of properties, which gradually increased in value.

In 1826, £48 was supplied by Sarah Greville's Charity (£24 from each parish) £13 from Thomas Oken's, £7 16sh. from Earl Brooke's and £1 12sh. from Fulke Weale's. This money was paid to the schoolmaster, presumably as joint income for his and his wife's services. The clothing appeared to be paid for separately and if the schoolmaster wished to have some private pupils, this was allowed.

The premises were maintained by the Town Corporation (King Henry VIII's Charity) and for the accommodation, the schoolmaster had to pay a nominal rent of 2 pounds a year, which was usually waived "in consideration of his (her) teaching at the charity school there."

From 1828 however, a new agreement meant that Samuel Gazey, the new schoolmaster, actually paid a tiny rent of 5 shillings a year.

A PENCIL SKETCH OF EASTGATE COMPLETED IN THE MID NINETEENTH CENTURY BY PHOEBE PARKES. The illustration is unusual in that a side view is shown and St Peter's Chapel looks more like a church. This sketch is one of several of the Warwick area contained in a scrapbook compiled by Miss Parkes between 1825 and 1850. (W.C.R.O.)

A QUIET CORNER OF THE BATTLEMENTS ON EASTGATE. This photograph was actually taken about 1970, but it could just as easily have been taken a hundred years previously. It is interesting to note that a tap exists in the corner between the door and the window and presumably this tap supplied the water for the entire building in earlier days. As this area lies close to the pedestrian arch on the Smith Street side, it often goes unnoticed.

Whenever extra items were needed, the charities usually provided extra funds. From 1817, Sarah Greville's Charity paid an annual sum for stationery and this usually amounted to £5 10sh. for each parish. In 1819 £1 16 6d had been paid by each parish on behalf of Mrs Greville's Charity, to pay for Bibles and Psalters for use by the pupils.

Road Changes. A New Bridge. Eastgate is Given a Facelift!

Huge changes were brought about in Warwick in the latter part of the Eighteenth Century.

Following the rebuilding of St Nicholas' Church in 1779–80 by Thomas Johnson of Warwick, other massive building operations were undertaken, providing much work for those in the construction business. In 1788, Eastgate was reconstructed and in 1789, a massive undertaking saw the building of a new bridge and a new road to Banbury. The design of the town was to change dramatically.

George Greville, Earl of Warwick offered to pay most of the cost of the new bridge which was desperately needed, if the new bridge was sited some distance away from the Castle, thus enabling more ground to be enclosed within the Castle walls. Previously the road into Warwick from the South had been via the village of Bridge End, over the old bridge (the remains of which are still visible near the Castle) past the end of Mill Street and into the town centre via Castle Street.

The bridge was begun in 1789 and opened in 1793, when new roads to serve it had been completed. These roads involved the demolition of some houses, but eventually linked a new straight section of the road to Banbury, with a route past St Nicholas' Church and up Back (now Castle) Hill to Eastgate. This obviously resulted in a tremendous increase in traffic either side of Eastgate, leaving it rather isolated. William Eboral, who had been responsible for the masonry of the bridge, also built the new walls around the Castle Grounds.

One wonders what the influential Landor family thought to all the building work, right on the doorstep of Landor House.

In many ways, the Eastgate may have been lucky to survive with a mere facelift. Had a flourishing charity school not been housed in St Peter's Chapel, it may have been a different story. There must have been some who thought it more logical to demolish the old gate and redesign the Jury Street and Smith Street junction, but had that happened, the school would have had to be found other accommodation, which might well have landed King Henry VIII's Charity (Town Corporation) in even more expense. So a reconstruction of Eastgate was probably the cheapest option.

Francis Hiorn Gets The Contract.

Having had his design for St Nicholas' Church turned down some years earlier, Francis Hiorn was given the consolation prize of redesigning Eastgate. Some idea of the work carried out can be gained by comparison of pictures of the building, before and afterwards. Considered a fine exponent of the fashionable Gothic style, Mr

EASTGATE PRE 1788 — From an oil painting attributed to the Circle of John Richards. This delightful scene showing masons at work in the foreground and a line of washing hanging above the town wall is now in a private collection.

Photograph by Simon Photography, Leamington Spa.

EASTGATE AROUND 1820.
This copper engraving of Eastgate was completed in the early Nineteenth Century by an unknown artist.
(As the streets appear to be paved, the date must be after 1811, but before 1826 when the extra schoolroom was built on the town wall.)
This engraving was included in a collection of 6 (Castle and town of Warwick) by Merridew & Son Ltd. (W.C.R.O.)

Hiorn made the boys' schoolroom over the roadway larger and added pinnacles to the roof and crenellations to the actual gateway. It would seem that rather than wholesale demolition, resurfacing and restructuring went on over a period of months.

The total cost was £382—a large sum of money in 1788. The account book of the King Henry VIII's Charity carries the details of 3 bills paid for "repairing the East Chapel and duty on materials." The first bill was for £7 0 5d and the other two together totalled £298 8 6d. In addition, Thomas Williams was paid £64 0 2d for the carpenters' work and James Marshall £13 9 11d for the Whitesmiths' work.

The Hiorn family had taken over the building firm begun by Francis Smith and later carried on by his son William. David and William Hiorn carried on a highly successful business and Francis, the son of William, carried on the family tradition.

Having been born in 1744, like his father, Francis became Mayor of Warwick several times. When only 29, Francis took office in 1773 and later he was Mayor twice again from 1782–3 and from 1787–8. Perhaps I am cynical, but I could not help reflecting that Francis was Mayor when his design for Eastgate was accepted.

However I feel sure that it was his fine reputation which had gained the contract. Previously Francis had worked on numerous buildings far afield from Warwick including St Ann's Church in Belfast, Hiorn's Tower near Arundel Castle and the stable block at Althorpe House (now with interesting connections with the Princess of Wales).

Sadly, Francis Hiorn died the year after the work on Eastgate was begun. He was only 45 at the time of his death in 1789, having survived his father by only 13 years.

I must confess, although there was an old world charm about the pre 1788 St Peter's Chapel, in general I prefer the Gothic additions made by Francis Hiorn. There is no doubt that he gave the old St Peter's Chapel a new lease of life. However the ornate additions to the Jury Street side of the archway were more controversial. Some of the work was heavily criticised as in the Gentleman's Magazine of 1801.

In an article entitled "The Pursuits of Architectural Innovation" the following remarks were made concerning the work on Eastgate.

> "But here some one or other has had the opportunity to show his contempt
> for ancient workmanship by his vanity in improving on those remains."

Strong comment! Perhaps it was just as well Francis Hiorn never read that.

A Successful School. A Complicated Shift System.

During the Nineteenth Century, the Bablake Charity School went from strength to strength. In 1819, the number of pupils was still the customary 75, but by 1833, there were 111 and by 1851, 130 scholars. The teaching appeared to be of a very high standard and private pupils were allowed to swell the ranks.

The boys and girls were taught separately and each followed a complicated timetable. In general the boys were taught the 3 R's—Reading, Writing and

EASTGATE AROUND 1821.
This photograph is of a watercolour included in the Aylesford Collection, now housed in Birmingham Reference Library. In an effort to document all the important buildings in Warwickshire, the Earl of Aylesford engaged a team of artists who worked for several years around 1821. The narrow pedestrian arch, before the additional schoolroom was built above, shows up well on this illustration. As one of the pinnacles is missing and also part of the roof, it would appear that the painting was unfinished.

Arithmetic, whilst the girls did reading, writing and sewing. However those girls on Mrs Greville's foundation were also taught arithmetic—by the master in the boys' schoolroom, when the boys were having a breakfast or lunch break.

The boys in the Charity School started work at 6 a.m. during the summer and 7 in winter. They worked till 5 p.m. with substantial breaks from 9 to 10 o'clock for breakfast and from 12 to 2 o'clock for lunch. The girls started at 9 a.m. and spent most of the day, being taught by the master's wife in their own room, apart from the periods when they were taught by the master in the vacant boys' room.

To complicate matters, there were other private pupils being given extra tuition at certain times. The proceedings sounded like a recipe for administrative chaos, but the teachers seemed to manage extremely well.

The Extensions.

In 1826, a new room was built for the girls on the section of old town wall, to the north of Eastgate. The 36 or more girls desperately needed a larger room and an entry in the King Henry VIII Charity Account Book for 1826/7 read,

> "Paid John Smyth a bill for erecting a room at St Peter's or the East Chapel for the benefit of the health of the scholars there."

The new room built for the 36 girls was around 16 feet by 14 feet, so if the previous room had been much smaller—no wonder their health had suffered! The new room cost £210 and was also supposed to double as extra accommodation for the schoolmaster's family.

At a later date, a further extension was built over the section of old town wall, more or less where the present extension to The King's High School is situated today.

The Teachers of the Bablake School.

In past centuries, most teachers, like other workers, remained in their posts until their death. Few could save from their meagre salaries and so had no means of support if they ceased to work. In the case of many teachers, their accommodation also went with the post, so they had a double incentive to continue, even if they were very old or ill. Very often, when new teachers were appointed, they were ex-pupils who had shown particular promise and had been offered the post of apprentice teacher, when they reached the Bablake School leaving age of twelve years.

In 1700 the charity school in Eastgate was taught by master Thomas Meads. The widow Morris taught for a number of years until her death in 1753. Between 1753 and 1789 when he died, the school master was Abraham Owen.

From 1789 onwards, the teacher was Mr Smyth, who had himself been educated at the Bablake School under Mrs Greville's Charity. Having been partly disabled by an accident in early life and not been thought fit for a more active occupation, the parish officers thought he ought to become a schoolmaster! For a while, he was sent to a superior school (Warwick School?) so that he could continue his own education, before returning to the Bablake School as master.

For nearly forty years, Mr Smyth ran the Bablake School, which gained an excellent reputation during this period.

In 1828, another former pupil became master when Samuel Gazey was appointed. Like John Smyth, Samuel Gazey had been educated in the Bablake School himself as one of Mrs Greville's scholars.

Born in 1799, from 1812 onwards, when aged 13 and too old to continue as scholar, he had acted as the Assistant Master. After 12 years, he had become the Master of Bishops Tachbrook School (a charity school founded in 1766) but he returned to Warwick on the death of Mr Smyth. The Gazey family had many connections with Tachbrook and perhaps through the influence of the Landor family, James Gazey, presumably a near relation, took over as master of the Tachbrook School.

In many ways, the influential Landor family were like local squires, giving their patronage to those they thought able. There had been Gazeys in Warwick for centuries and as Samuel had been born in Tachbrook, he had probably been known to the Savage family from birth. Henry Eyres Landor had been the Representative for Sarah Greville's Charity for the Parish of St Nicholas and presumably he used some influence to have Samuel Gazey appointed as the Master of Tachbrook in 1824. Certainly, Henry Eyres Landor was a member of the Charities School Board which appointed Samuel Gazey as Master of the Bablake School in 1828.

In actual fact, the appointment of Samuel Gazey was an extremely wise one and I think it would have appealed to the Landors that such an able local boy had received his just deserts.

For a number of years, as he had the reputation of being a fine teacher of basic subjects, Samuel Gazey gave extra tuition to private pupils, including some from the King's Grammar School, then housed nearby in The Butts. The curriculum of Warwick School in those days was centred on classics, like the other Grammar Schools, but Mr Gazey provided more modern tuition in basic subjects.

In his book, "A History of Warwick School" A. Leach quoted from an account given by an old Warwickian, Rev. James Baly, Archdeacon of Calcutta.

> "Such was the education given at Warwick School during my six years attendance from 1832 to 1838. It must not be supposed that we received no education in the items of writing, arithmetic and reading English. But we had to go elsewhere for it, to the master of the Bablake School, held in St Peter's Chapel, then Eastgate, from 8.30 to 9.00 and again from 12 to 1 o'clock, his disengaged hours."

A Tight Squeeze! The Census Returns.

I could not help laughing when I read the number of persons living in St Peter's Chapel in 1841. With perhaps 120 pupils in the school by day, if anything the living quarters were even more crowded by night. Apart from Samuel Gazey and wife Ann, both aged 40, there were their 4 children—Mary aged 15, Emma 13,

Alice 10 and George 5 years. John Etchells aged 15 was the Assistant Master and Mary Hart aged 14, the servant girl.

As if these 8 people were not enough, there were 2 servants, Thomas Hiorns and John Smith, both aged 25, living in an outhouse! Perhaps this outhouse was the extension to the Bablake School on the town wall? I presume that Thomas Hiorns was the servant later to inhabit the smaller cottage and marry three times. His name was either spelt Hirons or Hiorns and the age would tally with that in later Census Returns.

By 1851, only daughter Alice was listed as still living at the school, together with John E. Evans aged 17, a schoolmaster's apprentice. Eliza Evans, a servant girl from Milverton, completed the household.

By 1861, Samuel and Ann Gazey were aged 62 and daughters Mary Ann aged 35 and Alice aged 30, were Assistant Teachers. However by 1871, Ann Gazey was dead and Samuel and Alice had moved to 25 Jury Street, presumably to live with daughter Emma, aged 43, who kept a lodging house. (As there is no number 25 in Jury Street today, perhaps these premises were above the shop occupied by Elizabeth Rutherford?)

If one examines the accommodation in Eastgate today, it is a marvel that so many people over the years managed to live and work in the building. Where they all slept is a mystery, but the existence of a raised platform in the upper room would suggest that sections were subdivided. However in 1841, to fit eight persons into that meagre accommodation would take some doing.

Those Rough Bobdogs!

As might have been expected with two different schools situated close together, there was great rivalry between the boys of Warwick Grammar School and those of the Bablake School. The boys of the Charity School were often nicknamed "Bobdogs" and they had a reputation for being extremely tough. Mr Bowen, writing reminiscences in a school magazine years later wrote,

> "The costume of the boys attending the school (Bablake) consisted of a cap and coat similar to that worn by the Beefeaters, with knee-breeches and stockings. As their costume was old-fashioned, so were their manners. The few college boys who had to pass the Bobdogs School door daily on their way had an experience that must have hardened them for the rough and tumble of after life."

Excellent Education. Mr J. Dean (Senior)

In 1957, I was fortunate enough to interview Mr John Dean, a much respected Decorator and Signwriter, then aged nearly 80. Mr Dean told me that his father had attended the Bablake School around 1850.

The Deans lived in Castle Street and had been builders and decorators for many years. Mr Dean Junior told me that his father always spoke very highly of Mr

THE EASTGATE WHEN NATHANIEL HAWTHORNE, THE AMERICAN NOVELIST, VISITED WARWICK IN 1853. From 1853–7 Hawthorne was U.S. Consul in Liverpool and whilst visiting Warwick he witnessed a Military Parade, which this engraving was intended to record. Hawthorne visited many other towns and in 1857, resided at 10 Landsdowne Circus in Leamington for a while. Eastgate looks in good repair here as in 1847, much repair work had been carried out by I. and W. Bonehill, Stonemasons, for which they had been paid £223 16sh. (W.C.R.O.)

THE PEDESTRIAN ARCH UNDER EASTGATE. In 1826 when the extra schoolroom was built above, the tunnel was enlarged at a slightly different angle. Today this view is much photographed by visitors as the arch provides a most attractive frame for the Tudor cottages beyond.

THE GREEK DORIC PILLAR BOX NEAR EASTGATE.

This Victorian pillar box, cast in 1856 at the Eagle Foundry of Messrs Smith and Hawkes, Broad Street, Birmingham is one of the few remaining in England. One of a pair, a similar pillar box still remains near the West Gate in Warwick.

The drinking fountain was donated in 1859 by Richard Greaves, a Wilmcote quarry owner and previous mayor of the town. When first installed, this fountain must have been extremely popular with the thirsty pupils of the charity school held in St Peter's Chapel. Happily, it has recently been refurbished.

EASTGATE
A ROMANTIC SETTING FOR MUSIC
LESSONS.
This delightful window is situated in a small room, next to the main schoolroom, facing down Castle Hill. Having once possessed an outside chimney, it was previously the kitchen in the days when a family inhabited the building. In later years, it was used as a music room, many girls struggling through their piano exercises in ancient splendour!

THE STAIRS TO THE UPPER ROOM IN EASTGATE. This curving staircase, with windows which look into the two lower schoolrooms, is an emotive place. As you ascend the wooden stairs, polished by centuries of care and use, time seems to stand still.

Gazey, who was well-liked by the boys, despite being very strict concerning discipline. The education received by his father had been excellent and although he had only attended for a few years, he was perfectly literate and numerate.

Treats For the Schoolchildren.

Life in the Bablake School in the Nineteenth Century was not all hard grind, as there were occasional treats which gave the pupils some time away from their studies.

To start with each September there was the annual celebration of Oken's feast, when the whole school dined. No doubt this day was eagerly awaited by all pupils.

On 29th May 1856, at the conclusion of The Crimean War, a dinner for schoolchildren and old people was held on the race-course and on 16th June 1858, the pupils joined the boys from the Grammar School and the other Elementary Schools, to wave to Queen Victoria opposite the Castle Gates. Imagine the excitement as lines of boys and girls were marched down from Eastgate to the platforms provided for the children.

On 10th May 1863, there was a huge procession of 2,500 schoolchildren and others to celebrate the wedding of The Prince of Wales (afterwards King Edward VII) and Princess Alexandra of Denmark. After proceeding to the Common and singing the National Anthem, the children were given tea in their various schools.

When I want something cheerful to think about, I try to imagine the scene in Eastgate on that afternoon. Both schoolrooms would have crammed full of expectant children, clad in their old fashioned uniforms, eyes agog at the cakes and other unusual goodies provided for the occasion. I feel sure Samuel and Ann Gazey would have gone to some lengths to provide everyone with a treat to remember.

Closure of the Bablake School 1875.

When the Endowed Schools of Warwick were reorganised under a scheme of 1875, the Bablake School was closed. Government legislation in 1870 decreed that elementary education was to be available for all and it was felt it would be better to have newer schools in purpose-built premises. Under the Warwick scheme, the funds from the various charities supplying the Bablake School were diverted to the King's Schools; a new Boys' Middle School and a Girls' School being created alongside the old Boys' Grammar School. The only problem was that the three schools proposed were Secondary Schools and the Bablake School had provided many places for those in the younger age group seeking Elementary Education.

However, it was inevitable that the Bablake School would have to move sooner or later, as the premises had become inadequate for the number of pupils. The charity school held in St Peter's Chapel had served the town well for over 150 years but the old order was changing.

According to A. Leach in his "History of Warwick School" the old school bell was transferred to the new premises for the Boys' Grammar School in the Myton

A MODEL OF THE BABLAKE SCHOOL.

This model of Eastgate and the Bablake School was constructed by William Wallin, the Head Master of the school before it closed in 1875. The model was presented to the town of Warwick by William's son, Major Wallin and it is now part of the Town Museum, situated in the Vaults under the Court House. The extension on the left was demolished when the Bablake School was closed, but it would appear that the lower part of the wall was retained and is now incorporated into the entrance of the King's High School. (The model needed slight repair at the time of this photograph).

Simon Photography, Leamington Spa.

Road. As Fulke Weale had left money to provide the clock and turret on St Peter's Chapel, it seems likely that the school bell was inscribed "Ex dono Fulke Weale gen. 1730" as Mr Leach claimed.

In the Census Return of 1871, William Wallin was a Pupil Teacher, aged 19, living at 33 Theatre Street. However by 1874, he was running the Bablake School and was the last master. Some time after the school closed, Mr Wallin made a scale model of Eastgate, in order to show the old school premises. This model is carefully preserved in a glass case, which is kept in the Town Museum under the Court House.

EASTGATE DECORATED FOR THE DIAMOND JUBILEE OF QUEEN VICTORIA IN 1897. In 1887 Eastgate, together with the Court House and Westgate Chapel, had been illuminated with gas jets in coloured lamps which outlined the shape of the building. Ten years later it would appear that the same decorations were used again. The Adams family were living in the building at the time and their trim window box adds a homely touch. (W.C.R.O.)

The question is always asked—why was the charity school called the Bablake School? No-one ever seems to have come up with a satisfactory answer, but there

THE PENDULUM OF EASTGATE CLOCK. The size of the huge pendulum can be appreciated by comparison with the maintenance ladder also shown.

was probably some connection with the much older Bablake School in Coventry. That school seems to have had a connection with a Boys' Hospital, so perhaps the Warwick school was conceived with a similar idea in mind.

After the closure of the school, once again the building was converted into private accommodation. In 1880 Joseph Hobbs, a coachman was living there, but by 1881, Henry Adams, the Beadle and Town Crier, had moved in with his family. Henry was 26 years old and his wife Mary 24. The couple had a son Sidney aged 1 year and there was a servant girl Elizabeth Wills aged 14.

The Adams family continued to occupy the old chapel for a number of years. Later, they had at least one daughter, who attended the nearby King's High School For Girls.

Eastgate Clock.

Most clocks on public buildings were placed there in the mid nineteenth century, but the clock on Eastgate is far older than that.

In 1729, the will of Fulke Weale had provided money for the clock and turret on St Peter's Chapel, besides donating other money towards education. When Eastgate and St Peter's Chapel were reconstructed in 1788, the clock was presumably retained and modified. Superficially the new building looked different, but in reality it may well have been that much of the old building was retained.

Eastgate clock today bears the name 'Simmonds' and it may well have been installed by the firm of the same name whom Ann Johnson in Landor House had been paying to maintain her clocks and watches in 1732. From 1545, the maintenance of Eastgate and St Peter's Chapel had been the concern of King Henry VIII's Charity and there are many references in the Account Books to payments made to various clock-makers for cleaning and repairing the clock.

I was amused to read in the Account Books that for many years Samuel Gazey, the Master of the Bablake School for much of the nineteenth century, was paid 10sh 6d a year to wind and care for the clock. Perhaps this duty was generally carried out by the school master who lived on the premises?

Today Mr Miles, the present Caretaker of The King's High School, takes a great interest in winding the ancient mechanism and seeing that the correct time is shown. Following in the footsteps of Samuel Gazey and others, Mr Miles is paid a small annual fee for this extra task.

There have been several changes of appearance for the clock over the two and a half centuries that it has been in position. Pre 1788, the round clock face was set in a square surround, but after the reconstruction of the building, the surround was diamond-shaped. Around 1920 the clock was given quite a new look, when a round luminous face with no surround, was fitted. This was the face regilded by John Dean in 1956 and possible at other times also. Around 1968, various work was completed on Eastgate. The old chimneys were removed and a diamond-shaped clock surround, similar to that in the nineteenth century, was put in place.

LANDOR HOUSE BECOMES A SCHOOL.

Ladies' Seminary in 1858.

After the death of Elizabeth Landor, the house was cleared and first let to Miss Campbell, who died in 1855 and then to Mr J. Kershaw, who only remained for one year. The problem was that many of the gentry had deserted Warwick for Leamington and the old house was difficult to let.

However, the problem was solved in 1858 when Rev. Abraham Burdett, a Baptist Minister took the lease and his wife Caroline turned the premises into a boarding school for young ladies. Maybe the 52 year old Rev. Burdett was in ill health or semi-retired, for he was merely a member of the congregation, not the minister, at the nearby Castle Hill Baptist Church. Caroline aged 48, was listed as the Principal of the Ladies' Seminary and the couple's son Frank Laugham aged 14, was also living in the house.

The census of 1861 gave numerous details of the school. To assist Mrs Burdett, there were four young teachers—Rosabella Shakell aged 23, Emily Phillips aged 23, Charlotte Ibberson aged 23 and Jane Smith aged 19. There were four resident servants—Caroline Owen aged 21 was Cook and the three housemaids were Sarah French aged 21, Elizabeth Haynes aged 22 and Elizabeth Ford aged 20.

Twenty seven female scholars were listed, with ages ranging from 10 to 15 years. The girls appeared to have come from a wide variety of places for although some had been born in Warwickshire, others had been born in places as far afield as Burslem, Liverpool, Belfast, London and Australia.

So in Landor House at that time, there were only two males, but thirty six females. Poor Frank must have been overwhelmed!

Mrs Borton and Miss Marlin.

The Burdetts continued to rent Landor House until 1867 when Mrs Borton and Miss Marlin ran a different kind of school there.

From the Census of 1871, it appeared that apart from Sarah Borton, a widow aged 48 and her unmarried sister Anna Marlin aged 47, there were three other teachers. Louisa Long aged 19 was a teacher of French, Elizabeth Banger aged 32 taught Music and only Sarah Harvey aged 24 was listed as a general teacher, apart from the co-owners of the school.

When the list of nineteen pupils was examined, it was clear that the average age was higher than might have been expected. Although the ages of the scholars ranged from 12 to 23 years, the average age was around 16 and Cassie Borton, the 18 year old daughter of the co-owner, was herself a scholar.

The difference between the various classes of society was emphasized by the ages of the four resident servants. They were all young and only one of them was older than the oldest scholar. The aptly named Ellen Cooke aged 23 was Cook, Rebecca Green aged 18 was Parlourmaid, Mary Ann Watts aged 17 was Housemaid and Mary Anne Knight aged 14 was Under-housemaid. So the rich young ladies spent their time learning French and Music, whilst Mary Anne Knight had to leave her home at Shrewley, to enter service and spend her time working hard at numerous chores.

An Early Photograph of Landor House, taken in the 1860's. How different the adjoining cottage looks with the beams covered and tiny square window panes, instead of the iron lattice which replaced them. (W.C.R.O.)

This all female establishment in Landor House sounded very pleasant. I like to imagine the genteel young ladies in their long dresses, with voluminous petticoats, spending their time sketching some of the trees in the large garden, or practising the piano in one of the old panelled rooms.

The Gradual Run Down of the Property.

With the aging Landor House being used as a school, there was a gradual deterioration in the fabric of the building. As long as the wealthy Landor family had been prepared to help maintain the property, there was no problem, but with the Trustees having to pay for everything, there was conflict of interests. If too many repairs were done, there was little money to distribute to the poor.

During 1872, the Trustees decided to get estimates for repairs and for the sale of timber growing on the lawn of Landor House garden. In 1873, Mr Clarke paid £5 12sh for timber so some substantial trees must have been felled.

Also in 1873, the owners and occupiers of property in Chapel Street respectfully asked that the high wall in front of their houses might be lowered. The Trustees agreed and Mr Clarke removed 7,360 bricks which were sold. Today close inspection of the Chapel Street wall (or what remains) reveals the different levels.

In 1874, the old Potting House was pulled down and the once magnificent garden was gradually replaced by playground areas, more suitable for school use.

Education Needed Reorganization.

Throughout England in the latter part of the nineteenth century there was an enormous interest in education. In mid-century only half the children were educated at all and Secondary Education was unavailable to most. Many old fashioned Grammar Schools were in decline and the standard of elementary education provided by Endowed and Charity Schools was not always adequate. The nation's leaders realised that drastic measures were needed to ensure the future workforce received proper training.

A series of Acts of Parliament completely revolutionized education in England in the course of a few decades. The Puplic Schools Act was passed in 1867 and the Endowed Schools Act in 1869. In 1870 Forster's famous Education Act required Elementary Education to be available for all, although schooling was not compulsory till 1880 or free till 1891.

In Warwick as elsewhere, all schools were in the melting pot. Besides extra places in Elementary Schools, Secondary and Higher Education for girls was being demanded and the arguments were many.

The King's Grammar School Is Reorganised.

As early as 1864, a Schools' Enquiry Commission had urged that a greater share of Henry VIII's Charity be spent on education, in particular on improving the Grammar School.

As in many other towns, the Grammar School was in serious decline throughout the first few decades of the Nineteenth Century. The aged, gouty Headmaster George Innes had to remain in his post till his death in 1842 at the age of 82. With the study of Latin occupying a major part of the curriculum, it was small wonder that some pupils during the 1830s had attended the Bablake Charity School in Eastgate for extra tuition in more basic subjects.

Things did improve considerably at the Grammar School when the Rev. H. Hill was appointed Headmaster in 1843, but still the curriculum needed reforming. Controversy raged over this in the second half of the century. Some prominent citizens, led by Kelynge Greenway (afterwards the failed banker) favoured the traditional, classical approach, whereas others, notably Richard Child Heath, wanted modernisation. Both Mr Greenway and Mr Heath were Old Boys of the Grammar School, so much bitterness was created.

By 1870, it was obvious that great changes were coming and the wise and efficient Rev. Hill decided to split the King's Grammar School into two departments; the classical and the modern. The Classical Department remained in the school buildings in The Butts, under Rev. Hill, who remained overall Headmaster, but the Modern Department under F. Case, with an Old Boy W. Rainbow as Second Master, took up residence in Landor House.

The Account Books of Ann Johnson's Charity show that Rev. Hill was paying the £75 a year rent for Landor House from 1874 onwards. The arrangement seemed to work well, as the two premises were fairly close.

It would appear that not only was Landor House being used as a school by day, but evening classes in Arithmetic were also being held there. Nationwide it was realised that there was a need for further education, in particular evening classes for those workers who lacked basic skills. From 1874 onwards, Mr A.A. Corfe (Second Master of the Classical Department) gave regular lessons. The old panelled rooms, lit by candles or gaslight, must have provided a most romantic setting, quite out of character with the subject.

Proposals to Reorganise Secondary Education in Warwick.

In 1873 a draft scheme was put forward which proposed to close the Bablake Charity School and divert the funds into three new King's Schools; a new Grammar School, a Middle School for boys aged 10 upwards and a similar school for girls. New buildings would obviously be needed and the entire scheme was going to cost many thousands of pounds.

Most of the charities in Warwick wished to help and the Trustees of Ann Johnson's Charity were much involved from the onset. Since 1858, Landor House had been used as school premises and it must have occurred to someone (perhaps R.C. Heath?) that Landor House might be used to house one or two of the new schools. The house, which was in a run-down condition, would have been difficult to let as private accommodation, but with the house went a large amount of land suitable for redevelopment.

As early as 1873, there had been tentative enquiries concerning Landor House and no doubt the arrangements of 1874-6, when Rev. Hill officially rented the property, helped to further the cause.

A new site for the Grammar School was found on the Myton Road, so that was one school settled. However there was not sufficient money to buy land for the other schools and the old Grammar School buildings in The Butts were considered expensive to modernise.

Thus the involvement of Ann Johnson's Charity was crucial in the hunt for school premises. The Trustees were very sympathetic to the cause of Education, but on the other hand, the donation of property and/or large amounts of money would deprive the poor and needy of Warwick of much money to which they were legally entitled.

The Endowed Schools Reorganisation Scheme. 1875

Under the scheme eventually agreed in 1875, the three schools were to be set up in place of the King's Grammar School and The Bablake Charity School in St Peter's Chapel closed. The funds from the various charities were to be diverted into the main scheme, which it was hoped would benefit all the children of the town. It was proposed to award a few scholarships to each school, so that even the poorest children could have a chance of enjoying Secondary Education.

The new Boys' Grammar School was to have places for 250 boys, including 70 boarders and was to have new premises in the Myton Road, which would allow room for development. A new Boys' Middle School was to be created at a level above that of the new Elementary Schools, but below that of the Grammar School, with places provided for 100 boys, some of them boarders. In addition, there was to be a school for 80 girls; this school to be the counterpart of the Middle School For Boys.

The fees for the Boys' Grammar School were to be £6 to £12 per year, with boarders paying another £35. The Middle and Girls' School fees were to be £2 to £4 a year.

The funding was to come from many charities. The charities of Earl Brooke, Matthew Busby, Richard Edgeworth, Sarah Greville, Robert Heath, Fulke Weale and Sir Thomas Wheatley were combined and annual grants were received from Richard Griffin's, Thomas Oken's and King Henry VIII's Estate. The considerable income from Sir Thomas White's Charity was added every 4 years and in addition, there was the contribution from Ann Johnson's Charity.

Originally Ann Johnson's Trustees decided to grant £150 per year to the Schools' Reorganisation Scheme, but later it was decided to give Landor House and the cottages, instead of the annual rent of £105. To make up the shortfall, a further £50 each year would be given by the Charity.

Each of the Charities involved in the scheme was to appoint a certain number of Governors, but there were many disagreements. At one stage in 1875, Ann Johnson's Charity almost withdrew from the scheme altogether over a misunderstanding, but fortunately all was settled satisfactorily. This probably had much to do with the fact that in 1875 Richard Child Heath became one of the Trustees of Ann Johnson's Charity, besides Clerk to the Governors of the King's Schools. With a foot in both camps, Mr Heath was able to smooth over any difficulties which still remained.

A Formal Application For Landor House and the Cottages.

On 30th December 1875, Richard Child Heath, as Clerk to the Governors of the King's Schools, sent a formal letter to the Trustees of Ann Johnson's Charity.

> Dear Sir,
>
> I am directed by the Governors of the King's School to enquire whether the Trustees of Ann Johnson's Charity would be willing to part with the property fronting The Butts and Smith Street. The property in question, part of which is now let to Rev. H. Hill, expiring at Michaelmas next and the remainder is let to Mr J.T. Glover and another appears to the Governors to be desirable as the site for one of the Schools to be established. In case the Trustees should be willing to part with this property, perhaps you will kindly let me know as early as possible on what terms it can be acquired by the Governors.
>
> Yours truly,
> R.C. Heath.

The Trustees had to ask permission from the Charity Commissioners in London and before giving their answer, they asked for the premises to be valued. This was done in July 1876.

Valuation by J. Matthews of Waterloo Street, Birmingham.

> School House fronting street with outbuildings & dormitories on the side of Chapel Street and the whole of the back land used as playground and garden occupied by the Governors at a yearly rent of £75.
>
> House, buildings and Garden with shopping sheds and yards fronting Smith Street occupied by J.T. Glover at a rent of £24.
>
> House outbuildings and garden fronting Smith Street occupied by W. Highway at a rent of £6 yearly.
>
> Total Gross Rent – £105. The buildings generally are in a bad state of repair—especially the School House and premises.
>
> My estimate of the value of the whole is the sum of Fifteen hundred pounds. (£1,500)
>
> I am dear Sir
> Yours faithfully
> J. Matthews.

By December 1876, the Trustees of Ann Johnson's Charity had formally decided to hand the property to the King's Schools. This action was finalized in October 1877 and the building of the new premises for the Boys' Middle School was able to begin.

A Wise Decision By the Trustees?

In their application to the Charity Commissioners, the Trustees of Ann Johnson's Charity said they were,

> "Desirous of assisting in the establishment of the schools which it is believed will be of great benefit to the inhabitants of Warwick."

However there were many at the time and many since who felt that the Trustees made the wrong decision. The poor and needy of Warwick certainly lost out, when such a large sum of money (or property in lieu) was handed over to the Governors of the King's Schools. When I discussed the matter with him in 1957, Mr E.G. Tibbits, then Clerk to several charities, said he thought the Trustees in 1876 had been misguided. Ann Johnson left her property for a specific purpose and as long. as there were needy people in Warwick, any profits should have been given to them.

I recall Mr Tibbits speaking passionately against the transfer of the property and there can be little doubt that many poor people, over many years, were deprived of some extra income as a result. However in retrospect, I feel it was a brave decision by the Trustees as it ensured the long-term future of the houses. The property was difficult to let, apart from use for a school and although the poor undeniably lost out, many hundreds of pupils since that time have had the benefit of being educated in such emotive surroundings.

Rev. Herbert Hill.

One of the first casualties of the 1875 scheme was Rev. Hill, the Headmaster of the Grammar School since 1843. He had done much to revive the fortunes of the old school, but at Easter 1876, he was forced to retire to make way for a younger man to become Head of the remodelled school. In any case Rev. Hill did not think the new scheme was particularly wise. He felt that a town the size of Warwick could not sustain two fee-paying Boys' Schools, which were in direct competition with each other.

For several years, from 1873 onwards, Rev. Hill was a frequent visitor to Landor House and by all accounts he was a popular schoolmaster.

Having been born in 1810 and educated at Winchester and New College, Oxford, Herbert Hill was a fine classical scholar. Before being appointed Headmaster in Warwick, he had been Assistant Master at Rugby School for six years.

Besides being very efficient, he was popular with the boys and in 1846, when a burglar stole some of his silverware, a public subscription, with contributions from

Rev. Herbert Hill, Headmaster of Warwick School 1843–76. From 1874–76, he was leasing Landor House. Fond of reciting latin verses to himself, Herbert Hill was described by R. C. Heath as being "Tall and thin and of a grave and thoughtful countenance and when he smiled his face was transferred into a model of kindly intelligence." A popular Headmaster, he seems to have been an influential figure. (W.C.R.O.)

THE MIDDLE SCHOOL BUILDINGS IN THE BUTTS WHICH WERE BOUGHT BY ST MARY'S CHURCH COUNCIL IN 1910 AND RENAMED ST MARY'S CHURCH HALL. For many years, the organist lived in the Headmaster's House which is shown on the left. Following a serious fire in 1970, the house was demolished in 1977 and replaced by a block of flats. The rest of the buildings were demolished in 1981, after the site had been bought by the King's High School For Girls. This photograph was taken in 1975, when the premises were empty.
(W.C.R.O.)

scholars and parents, bought replacements. R.C. Heath had a high regard for Rev. Hill and corresponded with him regularly.

Herbert Hill married Bertha, a daughter of the poet Southey. She died in 1877 and in 1880, he was offered the prestigious post of Master of the Lord Leycester Hospital. He remained there until his death in 1892, at the age of 82 and although he was buried in Warwick Cemetry, there is a fine memorial cross to his memory and that of his wife, in the Nave of St Mary's Church, near the Regimental Chapel.

The King's Middle School.

From the onset, The Middle School was a success. Immediately after the retirement of Rev. Hill, the Modern Department, then occupying Landor House, provided the nucleus of pupils for the new school. Officially, from May 1876, the Middle School occupied Landor House under the newly appointed Headmaster

Rev. Willacy, a 26 year old who had previously been Assistant Master at Lancaster Grammar School. Nicknamed "Old Bird", he soon became a respected local character.

The new buildings were ready for occupation by July 1878 and around 72 pupils vacated Landor House. Sited on part of the garden, the buildings were more or less opposite to the Grammar School building in The Butts. Costing £2,638 apart from the tower, which was the gift of Alderman T. Dale, the new buildings included a large room, 50 feet by 20 feet, three classrooms and a workroom in the basement. The adjoining house for the Headmaster was substantial, with five bedrooms, so that boarders could be accommodated if required. There was a good sized garden to the house and a large ashphalt playground was provided for the boys.

In July 1878, the Warwick Advertiser carried a report concerning the move, which made me smile.

"For some time the scholars attending the King's Middle School have undergone their tutilage in the Eastgate House at the top of Smith Street, which, although spacious as a private residence, is not well adapted for scholastic purposes".

For a building not well suited to scholastic purposes, it is interesting to reflect that Landor House has been part of a school continuously since 1858.

The opening ceremony for the new buildings was on 1st August 1878 and the proceedings, as described by the Warwick Advertiser, sounded typically Victorian.

"The boys occupied a position opposite the platform and with Mr F. Spinney presiding at the harmonium, sang a number of hymns in a very creditable manner."

At the opening ceremony, R.C. Heath, as Clerk to the Governors, was much in evidence. He officially handed over the key to the Headmaster and the Mayor, Alderman Tibbits M.D. made a speech.

Mr G. J. Dean

Once again Mr G.J. Dean was able to help with some reminiscences. He had attended the Middle School from 1888-1892 and although the school was essentially a fee-paying school, there were 8 keenly contested scholarships, one of which he had won at the age of 10.

Interestingly enough, Mr Dean said that almost all the winners of the scholarships came from the Board Schools and some felt that perhaps Church Schools concentrated too much on Religious Education. The scholarships were valid for a period of 3 years, after which the parents of the pupil could pay if they wished their son to receive further education.

An old Middle School prize-list possessed by Mr Dean showed that the school offered a wide range of subjects including Latin, French, English, Mathematics (with Algebra and Geometry) History, Geography, Physics, Chemistry, Biology, Drawing and Music. Extra tuition in commercial subjects such as shorthand, and also piano lessons, could be had for the payment of a guinea a term. Homework was given each night and it seemed that the Middle School offered excellent education, even when judged by the standards of a century later.

The Girls' School Least Important?

Although the three new schools were supposed to share resources, there was an obvious inequality concerning the preparations. Both Boys' Schools had new purpose-built premises, but the Girls' School had to wait four years until Landor House became available. In 1875, well over forty years before any women had the right to vote, there were many who felt that Secondary Education for girls was quite unnecessary anyway. It was fortunate that the Girls' School had an articulate, well-respected advocate in R.C. Heath.

When Landor House fell vacant in 1878, work was done in readiness. With the Boys' Schools each costing thousands of pounds, all the Girls' School had was £446 spent on repairs and improvements to the old house.

In August 1879, the new buildings for Warwick School were opened and the old College buildings in The Butts were vacant. There was some talk of the girls moving there, but the idea was rejected and the King's High School For Girls became firmly established in Landor House.

The Later History of the Cottages.

Number 1, Smith Street, the larger cottage, appeared to have been occupied by the Salloway family for around ninety years. Soon after the cottages were separated, on the closure of the inn, the Salloway family firm of carpenters moved into the premises. Numerous people worked in the yard and various family members lived in the house.

In 1851, William Salloway, aged 56, was living there with his wife Hannah, who was ten years older than her husband. Apparently, the couple had no children and it was more than likely that William Salloway had been born in the cottage. The carpentry firm was obviously very well-respected and during the first half of the nineteenth century, often carried out work for Warwick Corporation.

William Salloway died in 1859, aged 64 and the long family tenancy ended. After extensive repairs, the buildings were offered to James Thomas Glover, a coach builder, then living in The Butts, who agreed to pay a rent of £23 per year, an increase of £15 on that paid by the Salloways.

James was aged 41 and his wife Susannah 40, when the family moved in later in 1861. The couple had six children including Harriet aged 12, twins Tom and Henry aged 11, Eliza aged 8, Annie aged 4 and Mary Ann, a baby of 12 months. The old cottage must have been bursting at the seams! With the noise of ten people employed in the coachbuilding yard outside and six children inside, it must have been a very busy place indeed.

Business must have prospered for by 1871, 20 men and 4 boys were being employed and son Tom had joined the family firm. Some of the Directories of the time carried advertisements for the carriage manufacturing firm. It appeared that additional premises in Leamington were also being used, so not all 24 employees were crammed into the yard near Eastgate.

THE HALLWAY OF THE LARGER COTTAGE — NUMBER ONE, SMITH STREET. In 1861 the Glover family with six children aged from 12 years to 12 months were pattering down this hallway. Several decades ago, the stairs on the left led to the Cottage Library and Miss Naish's form-room.

AN UNUSUAL VIEW OF THE LARGER COTTAGE.

Number 3, the smaller cottage, was let to the Bullock family for many years after 1769 and in the early nineteenth century, the Robinson family took the lease. When Joseph Robinson and his wife died, unmarried daughter Mary took over the lease, paying £4 10sh per year. The 1851 Census revealed some harsh statistics concerning the three inhabitants. Both Mary Robinson, the 58 year old Head of Household and Sarah, her 19 year old unmarried niece, gave their occupation as 'laundress'. It sounded as if the two women took in washing. The third inhabitant was Sarah, the 64 year old sister of Mary, who was classed as being "deaf, but not dumb."

From 1852, the cottage was inhabited by the Hirons (Hiorns) family. Thomas Hirons was Butler to Elizabeth Landor until her death in 1854. Thomas seemed to have had an eventful life for he had been married three times. By his first wife Ann, he had a son John, who became a printer's compositor. His second wife Judith bore sons Edward and William and his third wife Harriet bore another son Arthur. At varying times, some of the children were inhabiting the cottage.

During 1871, the rent of £4 10sh was increased by the Charity Trustees to £6 10sh per year, with the rather curt note that if Thomas Hirons refused to pay the extra, he was to be given notice to quit. The Census of 1871 revealed that the Hirons family had taken in two lodgers, Francis and Henry Flay, both young Cabinet Makers, presumably to recoup some of the extra rent.

Thomas Hirons died in 1881, aged 64 and his widow Harriet had to take in washing in order to make a living for herself, son Arthur aged 13 still at school and step-daughter Elizabeth aged 19, a general servant out of work. That household did not sound a prosperous one and it was small wonder that Sylvester Richardson, aged 47, was a lodger.

After 1877, when the ownership of the cottages had been passed, along with Landor House, to the King's Schools Foundation, both continued to be let. The separate occupation of the cottages continued until 1883, when The King's High School For Girls enlarged its premises and various building work was completed.

1879 ONWARDS. THE KING'S HIGH SCHOOL FOR GIRLS.

The King's High School For Girls opened in Landor House in the Spring of 1879. In June, when the first pupils were admitted, there were only 22 girls on the roll, but encouraged by such people as Richard Child Heath, the Clerk to the Governors, the school soon prospered. Within a few years, extra classrooms were being built and the number of pupils increased rapidly.

Miss Fisher—First Headmistress.

In February 1879, Mary Janet Fisher, aged 22, was appointed Headmistress from a short-list of five candidates. The Governors certainly made a wise choice, although she was very young.

Mary Fisher had been born and brought up in the West Ham district of East London, then classed as part of Essex. Although rather run down today, in those days, parts of West Ham were considered quite genteel and the proximity of the Borough to the Royal Docks and the City of London meant that it was a fashionable, bustling place.

Mary Fisher was well qualified, having been a student of the City of London College and holding the Higher Certificate of the University of Cambridge. She had previously been an Assistant Teacher at West Ham High School For Girls, which was an old charity school reopened in new buildings in 1876. The West Ham buildings were typically late Victorian, with a solid, two storey, purpose-built block being enclosed behind elegant railings. How quaint Landor House and Warwick must have seemed after that. In 1879, there were not even any horse-drawn trams in Warwick, never mind the ocean-going liners of West Ham!

Miss Fisher's salary was £100 per year, plus free residence. Furniture was provided, but earthenware was only provided in the bedrooms! Miss Wakefield, the Assistant Mistress also had a bedroom in Landor House, but £5 per year had to be paid. One of the attic rooms was adapted as a Music Room and the housekeeper had another upper room, but she supplied her own furniture.

The Census of 1881 revealed that Landor House had six female residents. The Headmistress Mary Fisher, then aged 24, had her married sister Emily Moore, aged 29, as Music Mistress in the school. Elizabeth Wakefield, born in Witney and aged 29, was the Assistant Mistress. The two resident servants were Susannah Grant, the unmarried Housekeeper aged 47 and Mary (Lei?) a general servant aged 17 and

MISS FISHER (MRS KELSON)
This attractive young women from West Ham in East London was the first Headmistress of the King's High School For Girls. She was appointed in 1879, but resigned in 1895 after several bouts of ill health.

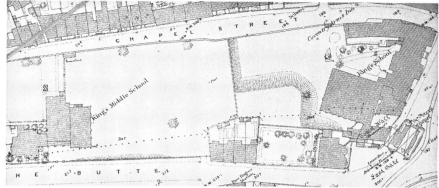

THE SITE AS SHOWN ON THIS ORDNANCE SURVEY MAP OF 1887 still has a few patches of garden left. The Headmaster's house to the left of the King's Middle School had a sizable garden extending to Chapel Street and near Landor House (shown to the right) there is a patch which still remains today. The Hall and Butts Entrance for The King's High School had been completed and although the smaller cottage had been incorporated into the Girls' School, the larger cottage was still a separate dwelling. The famous Ilex tree can be clearly identified in the Middle School playground, above the Parish Boundary line. (W.C.R.O.)

born in Dublin. Florence Bentley, aged 17, was classed as a visitor, although she later became a pupil-teacher at a salary of £15 per annum.

Later in 1881, space became so short for the ever growing number of girls that Miss Wakefield was asked to vacate her room, her salary being raised accordingly. In February 1882, space was still urgently required so temporarily, even Miss Fisher was asked to give up her rooms in Landor House. In that year, the old house must have been bulging, with the pupils still entering by the front door and using the stairs near the present Headmistress's Study to reach the classrooms on the first floor.

Those early years of the King's High School must have been very interesting, with every available room being used. According to various accounts, Miss Fisher allowed the older girls to visit the underground passage as a special treat on her own birthday and many girls took gifts of flowers to her room to celebrate the occasion.

In 1883, the school extended its premises considerably, the cottages being used for the first time as part of the school. Previously, they had continued to be let out to private tenants such as the Hirons family. In 1883, Mrs Hirons left the smaller cottage (presumably evicted) and the dividing wall from Landor House was partly demolished. For some years, the larger cottage nearest Eastgate continued to be separate and the School Caretaker and his family resided there.

Also in 1883, The Butts Entrance was constructed through the stone wall near Eastgate and the Hall and some new classrooms were built in the garden nearby.

Landor House Is Officially Named In 1892.

When I was conducting my research, much confusion was caused because until

*THE KINDERGARTEN DEPARTMENT IN THE LARGE UPPER ROOM IN
LANDOR HOUSE IN 1902. Once two bedrooms, the dividing wall was removed in 1880. The
window overlooks the back of the house and the remaining patch of garden and the door on the
right leads to the main staircase. This room is now a Staffroom.*

1892, Landor House was officially known as 'Eastgate House' which is now the
name of a house in Jury Street. I decided that to avoid misunderstanding, I would
refer to Landor House throughout my work, but the change of name is none the less
important.

In the Minute Book of The King's High School, I was interested to read how the
change of name came about.

On 16th November 1892, the Governors declared,

> "In consequence of the confusion arising from another house in the
> neighbourhood being called Eastgate House, it was resolved that the name
> of the School House be altered to Landor House."

This was a very wise decision by the Governors as the long association of the
premises with the Landor family became officially recognised and the school

benefited from having a scholarly sounding address, in keeping with the plaque above the front door.

The Final Years of Ann Johnson's Charity Before Amalgamation.

Although Landor House, the cottages and the extensive grounds had been given to the King's Schools, the Charity Trustees were still concerned in a minor way with the site. One of the conditions of the gift was that a representative of the Charity Trustees should be nominated as a school governor. From 1877 onwards, for a number of years that Charity Representative was Lord Brook and he does seem to have worked very hard on behalf of both organisations.

Hogbrook Farm had also been sold in 1877, so from that time onwards, all the Charity Trustees had to do was dole out money to the poor (the interest on the £6,000 invested by the Charity Commissioners after the sale of the farm). As always, each trustee had an equal sum to give to the poor and most years there was around £200 to be divided. This was a sizable sum, but although around 1880, there was an impressive list of seven trustees, the records kept were most uninteresting. In 1888, all the Earl of Warwick wrote in the charity account book was "22 poor persons at 2/6 each"

Like most organisations, Ann Johnson's Charity had lost money in 1887 when the Warwick Bank of Greenway, Smith and Greenway crashed. The Charity lost £161 16sh 2d and one of the failed bankers Kelynge Greenway had been one of Ann Johnson's Trustees. He resigned as Trustee and after prosecution was sentenced to one year's hard labour, as punishment for his poor management and dishonesty. His brother Charles got five year's penal servitude and there was a huge scandal and public outcry as hundreds of ordinary people found they had lost their money. Even the Warwick General Rate had to be increased to 3d in the pound, to recoup some of the losses of the public funds.

For some years the Trustees of Ann Johnson's Charity continued to hand out subscriptions to the Cottage Hospital (10 guineas) and the Warnford Hospital (14 guineas) and bread was still being provided in all four Warwick parishes (£2 12sh per year). However the old order was changing and in 1907, it was felt appropriate to merge Ann Johnson's Charity with several others.

On 9th December 1907 at 12 noon the last meeting of the Trustees of Ann Johnson's Charity took place. Those present were Mr H. Pratt, Mr J. Mellor, Mr J. Ward and Mr R.C. Heath as Chairman. There was a transfer of some investments to the King's Schools Foundation to make up for the loss of the £50 annuity. The balance of money remaining was transferred to the United Charities of Richard Griffin, John Talloos and Ann Johnson. Years later in 1956 after further amalgamations, the name was changed to The United Charities of Richard Griffin and others.

In after years, these united charities helped to provide housing for needy people, but perhaps the greatest Epitaph to Ann Johnson's Charity was Landor House— still used and loved by many pupils of The King's High School.

The School of Science and Art. The Technical School.

During the latter years of the nineteenth century, Technical Schools were being encouraged and many pupils attended 'Night School' in an effort to further their education, after they had left Elementary School.

In 1896, the Middle School underwent some reorganisation and it became incorporated in the School of Science and Art, which also catered for pupils beyond the school leaving age. Over £2,700 was spent on an extension containing a new Chemistry Laboratory and Lecture Theatre, with Art and Woodwork rooms above.

Once again Mr Dean was able to supply some first hand information. He said that after he left the Middle School he attended evening classes in the Technical School, in order to learn Signwriting and Lettering. It was in these classes that he learned the skills necessary to tackle such work as the repainting of the clock faces on Eastgate and Westgate.

Middle School Amalgamates With Grammar School 1906.

The misgivings which Rev. Hill had had in 1875 proved correct and within thirty years the two Boys' Schools had merged. The town could not support two similar schools and the Middle School, with lower fees, had prospered at the expense of Warwick School. So in 1906 the decision was taken to unite the Boys' Schools, under the Middle School Headmaster Mr H.S. Pyne, a graduate of Trinity College, Dublin. The Middle School moved to the Myton Road site, which meant that the extensive premises in The Butts were vacant.

The most sensible thing for the Governors to have done was give the Middle School buildings to the expanding Girls' School, but for some reason they insisted on selling to the Vicar and Churchwardens of St Mary's Church. The large site comprising 2,870 square yards, with substantial buildings, including the Headmaster's House, was valued at £2,200 and the Governors appeared to want to recoup some cash. St Mary's Council was keen to acquire the property but had some difficulty in raising the money. On 5th July 1911, a famous Garden Party held in the Castle Park attempted to raise enough money to cover the deficit still owing from the sale in 1910.

The buildings were renamed St Mary's Hall, but almost from the start the premises were too large for exclusive church use. For a few years, the Technical School, which was supported by a special grant from the County, continued to operate in the newer extension block. This arrangement went on until 1918, when the Technical School finally closed.

The Junior Department of the King's High School moved into the premises vacated by the Technical School and as the years passed, more and more rooms were leased to the Girls' School.

Richard Child Heath.

Throughout the second half of the nineteenth century, one man seemed to play a vital role in the administration of the site—the lawyer Richard Child Heath.

THE BUILDING IN THE CENTRE ONCE HOUSED THE 'WARWICK TECHNICAL AND ART SCHOOL'. In 1918, when the school closed, the building was leased to the Junior Department of The King's High School For Girls and later many other rooms in St Mary's Hall were also similarly leased. This photograph was taken shortly before demolition in 1981.

Born in 1833, Richard was the son of Thomas Heath, a well known lawyer who had been Town Clerk of Warwick. Having been educated at Warwick School, Richard had been Head-Boy in 1847. After graduating from University College, London, he later qualified as a lawyer.

From 1854 to 1871, Richard Heath was Under Sheriff of Warwickshire and as such was responsible for carrying out arrangements for executions. He attended many notable trials and his attention to detail made him a highly successful holder of the office.

Like his father, Richard Heath had extensive business interests and for a time was Chairman of Warwick Gas Company. He had a special interest in Voluntary Military Associations and he founded Warwick Boat Club, which represented another passion of his.

His career might have been even more illustrious had not Richard and his father had connections with the Liberal Party. In late Victorian times, politics played a great part in advancement.

Perhaps because he married the widow of Dr Blenkinsop and had four daughters, but no sons, Richard long championed the cause of Higher Education for girls.

RICHARD CHILD HEATH WHO WAS CLERK TO THE GOVERNORS OF THE KING'S SCHOOLS FROM 1875 TO 1906. His shrewd and sensible attitude helped a great deal with the reconstruction of Warwick School and the creation of The King's High School For Girls. It was said of him "Warwick School never had a more loyal Old Boy." He never ceased to be interested in the Girls' School and he regularly attended the Prize-giving until his death in 1913. (W.C.R.O.)

THE SCHOOL HALL A FEW YEARS BEFORE THE ARRIVAL OF MISS DOORLY.
Most appropriately, a photograph of R. C. Heath is displayed centre stage, underneath the clock.
Despite the pictures, the atmosphere seems very formal and forbidding.

When he became Clerk to the Governors of the King's Schools during the difficult period from 1875 onwards, he took a particular interest in the King's High School For Girls.

From 1875, until his death on 12th July 1913 aged 80, he was a frequent visitor to Landor House and he was very supportive of the first two Headmistresses. Had he not been sympathetic to the cause of girls' education, the success of The King's High School For Girls might not have been so rapid. It would have been extremely difficult for Miss Fisher and Miss Lea to expand the school without a sympathetic official to ensure sufficient finance.

For many years, a photograph of Richard Child Heath hung in the Hall of the King's High School and it would appear that the girls owed him a great debt.

The Garden Disappears.

Since 1858, when Landor House first became a school the old house has been modified and new buildings have been constructed in the garden. Today, the once large garden, so loved by the Landor family, has all but disappeared, with only a few isolated pockets remaining.

By all accounts, a very old mulberry tree, probably dating from the time of the Landors, if not the Johnsons, was still in the section of garden near the present Staff Room until around 1930. Now what would seem to be a replacement mulberry tree stands tall and healthy, but hemmed in by new buildings. It is said that the Modern Languages Block, recently completed in 1991, was specially designed to allow the mulberry tree to remain.

A SAD SIGHT IN 1981. The demolition of St Mary's Hall provided a dramatic sight. Miss E. Tibbits, a long-standing resident of the road remarked recently, "I was sorry when the Middle School buildings were demolished. Somehow they lent character to The Butts." Today all that remains is a section of the distinctive front garden wall, near the pavement.

As many would find the details of various buildings extremely dull, a list is probably the best idea. Over the years, the interiors of Landor House and the cottages have become changed, but any conversions have been handled sympathetically, with the antiquity of the buildings borne in mind.

The King's High School For Girls Enlarges Its Premises.

(A Summary of Some of the Changes To the Site.)

1879   The school opens in Landor (then Eastgate) House.
1880   The playground completed. (Gravel donated by Lady Charles Percy from Guys Cliffe Fields)
         Two internal walls in Landor House removed.
1883   The Hall, extra classrooms and Butts entrance built.
1888   "Landor Born 1775" sign erected over front door.
1889   Two additional classrooms built at end of Hall.
1892   Landor House officially named. (Previously Eastgate House)
1902/3 Demonstration Room, Laboratory and Art Room built over additional classrooms.

DINE IN SPLENDOUR!
In the early years of the Twentieth Century, this elegant room was used as a dining room for the
girls. Now the Head Teacher's Study, this room was once a Parlour.

1905   Bicycle sheds in playground.
1906   Gymnasium of old Middle School taken over in playground. Adapted and
        used as Cookery and Botany/Biology Rooms.
1908   Dining Room built—old North wing of Landor House partly demolished.
        (Old Brewhouse, additional kitchen etc)
1916   Eastgate leased from King Henry VIII Charity.
1918   Inside staircase to Eastgate.
1947   Dining Hall extended.
1952   Remainder of old gas lighting replaced.
1954   Red Corridor built to classrooms and Dining Room.
1960   Two additional classrooms built near "Red House" garden, on site of old
        Air-Raid Shelters (built 1939)
1963   Adjacent "Red House" purchased.
1966/7 Tunnel entrance to playground. New Gymnasium etc.
1970   Bursar's Office built in Cottage Cloakroom.
        Serious fire damages rooms in St Mary's Hall.
1981   School buys back site of old Middle School. Remains of buildings

demolished. (St Mary's Hall, Old Technical School)
1991   Modern Languages Block built alongside Chapel Street.

Loyalty Much in Evidence.

It is interesting to speculate why so many teachers and other employees spent so much time connected with the King's High School. Until I began my research, I had no idea that so many employees had spent so many years with the school. To have worked on the site for 25 years was by no means uncommon and many caretakers, domestic staff and teachers seemed to have spent all their working lives helping the school.

Even the trades people who visited remained loyal over many years, building up a fine tradition of continuity. Of all the trades people who visited, surely none were more loyal or helpful than Mr John Dean, whose firm carried out the decorating. I do not know how long John Dean was connected with Landor House and the other buildings, but it must have been well over 50 years.

George John Dean.

John Dean was not only able to assist me concerning memories of the Bablake and King's Middle School, he was also a great character, who contributed much to Warwick. As Head of a highly respected decorating firm, he was a frequent visitor to the King's High School For Girls over many years and he did much to help preserve the fabric of the historical buildings.

Widely known as Jack, John Dean came from a skilled family of builders and decorators, his grandfather having been a decorator in Warwick in 1808. John was born in 1878, only two doors from Number 9, Castle Street, the house he inhabited for many years (now demolished).

After leaving school, John joined the family firm and in 1904, he married Gertrude Claymore in Leamington. During his professional life, he was a highly popular man, his integrity making him an ideal choice for a leader. For a time, he was President of the Building Trades Association for the Leamington and Warwick area and also a Provincial Master of the Manchester Unity of Oddfellows.

For much of his life, he was a member of the choir at St Mary's and he was a Sunday School Teacher for the amazing period of 71 years. Mr Reg. Barton, a long serving employee of The King's High School, had plenty of memories concerning John Dean.

"I was in his Sunday School class and afterwards he offered me a job," recalled Mr Barton recently. "I became apprenticed to him."

Apparently, it was not uncommon for John Dean to help his scholars find work.

Amongst other positions, John Dean had been Vicar's Warden at St Mary's and a manager of Borough Church School. For many years he acted as Trustee for several charities and also as Receiver for St Mary's Almshouses.

"A true craftsman of the old school". This great compliment was paid by the Vicar at John's funeral. Being a highly skilled signwriter, many of the difficult jobs fell to his lot. In 1953, the public spirited 75 year old volunteered to repaint the figure of Justice and the Royal Coat of Arms on the Court House, free of charge, as a contribution to the celebrations for the Coronation of Queen Elizabeth II. He still worked at heights when over 80 years old and his philosophy was that,

"If one acts old, then one is old!"

When visiting the King's High School recently, I spoke with a painter who had also been apprenticed to John Dean. Mr Peter Fretwell recalled that Mr Dean had been "A wonderful boss," and there is not much higher praise than that!

Apparently having no children of his own, John Dean seemed to love children and on his eightieth birthday, he celebrated by having a party for 60 children in St Mary's Hall. It seemed most appropriate that the same hall had had once been part of the King's Middle School, where he had been educated.

Having been a widower for many years, when he retired from his position as Sunday School Teacher in 1964, when aged 86, John Dean was given an unusual gift. The church members clubbed together and presented him with a divan bed which was far more comfortable than the bed he had been using. What a sensible gift!

I count myself very fortunate to have been given an interview by John Dean in 1957, when I was an enthusiastic college student and he was nearly 80. I recall with pleasure the afternoon I spent with this polite, upright gentleman, who made me tea and chatted for hours about the Warwick of his youth.

When he died on 15th December 1965, aged 87, Warwick lost one of its most caring citizens. It says much for his character that he is still well-remembered today.

The Ilex Tree.

One of the most famous trees in Warwick must have been the old Ilex tree, which was left when the playground of the Middle School was constructed around it. Certainly, Walter Savage Landor and his family must have sat beneath its shade and later on hundreds of Middle School scholars used to climb it and sit on the branches.

Although the tree may have been there in earlier years, it would seem probable that it was planted early in the Nineteenth Century by members of the Landor family. Walter Savage Landor spent much time in the Florence area of Italy, where such "evergreen oaks" were common. Walter and his sisters were keen gardeners and often exchanged seeds and plants. Walter loved trees in particular and took a great interest in the Warwick garden, where he once mentioned a nightingale which must surely have perched on the Ilex tree.

When a magazine was started in 1911 by pupils of the King's High School For Girls, the name "Ilex" was chosen for it. I do not know who chose the name, but

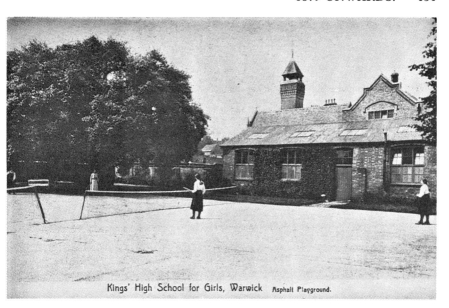

Kings' High School for Girls, Warwick   Asphalt Playground.

THE FAMOUS ILEX TREE LOOKING HEALTHY AROUND 1918.
To the right can be seen the old Middle School buildings, which had been purchased by St Mary's
Church Council in 1910. The creeper clad ex-gymnasium in the foreground was used as Biology
and Cookery Rooms by the King's High School For Girls.

whoever did made an inspired choice, for no advertising executive, paid thousands of pounds for her judgement, could have made a finer choice. For generations of pupils of King's High School, the name conjured up all that was fine, unchanging and worth remembering about the past.

When the famous old tree finally crashed to the ground one Autumn afternoon in 1949, there were many who were extremely sad. True for a number of years, branches had had to be propped up and railings placed around it, but no-one ever expected it to die. As I was close by when it happened, I well remember the eerie crash as it blew over, partly crushing some bicycle sheds.

Eventually the tree was removed by Mr Gardner, a local woodcarver, who made souvenirs such as bowls and egg-cups, after the wood was properly seasoned, several years later. Like many others, I really loved the old tree, but I did not buy any of the bowls. However when I read about Walter Savage Landor having a writing desk made as a 70th birthday present out of the wood of his favourite Warwick cedar tree, after it had blown down in a gale, I wished I had bought something. The Ilex souvenirs were carrying on a fine tradition.

Eastgate in the Twentieth Century.

For the early years of the century, the Adams family continued to occupy the old chapel building. Amongst his other official duties, Mr Adams was the Mace Bearer.

Kings' High School for Girls, Warwick The Library.

EASTGATE — THE ADDITIONAL SCHOOLROOM OVER THE PEDESTRIAN ARCH.
Built in 1826, this room was once the Girls' Room, where 36 pupils attending the Charity School were educated. The photograph seems to have been taken between 1918, when Eastgate was first used by the Senior School and 1922, when the Library was transferred to the upper room. Interestingly, the larger picture helps to hide a doorway to the battlements.

However in 1916, once again St Peter's Chapel became a schoolroom. The property, which was still maintained by the Trustees of King Henry VIII's Estate, was leased to the King's High School For Girls. A token rent was charged and a long lease was agreed.

At first the Kindergarten used the building, access being provided by the same old stone steps used for centuries. However, after a few terms, the Junior Department moved to the old Technical School buildings and the main school was able to use the property. In 1918, a new inside staircase was constructed, linking the old rooms with a nearby corridor and the teachers and older girls used the rooms for a number of years.

Until the end of the Second World War, the large room above the road arch was used as a staff room. During the war years, the staff fire-watchers used this room at night, as it provided an excellent vantage point.

In 1945, when boarding ceased in the school, all the rooms in the older buildings were reorganised and Eastgate provided several Sixth Form rooms. Such was the shortage of space in the years following the war, even the small room which had once been the kitchen was used as a music room.

The Kings High School for Girls, Warwick. The Library.

EASTGATE IN THE TIME OF MISS DOORLY.

The upper room, then used as a Sixth Form Library, has delightful old beams supporting the ceiling. In the days prior to 1916, when a family inhabited the building, this room was probably subdivided to form several bedrooms. To the right of the door, shown on the right of the photograph, a raised area of polished wood would seem to mark the site of an inner room.

It was not only the staff fire-watchers who used Eastgate as a vantage point. For many years, the battlements provided girls with an excellent spot from which to watch processions in Jury Street, Castle Hill or Smith Street.

On 14th June 1923, some of the pupils clad in white frocks, had a wonderful view of the Prince of Wales as he was slowly driven up Smith Street. Once again the battlements came in useful at the end of the Second World War, when the girls were able to wave to Field Marshal Montgomery as he drove past during the Victory celebrations. I presume it was a Sixth Form privilege to be allowed onto the battlements on such occasions—there could not have been room for too many girls.

Although the trams had always travelled round Eastgate, other traffic had the option of going through the ancient gateway. On numerous occasions, lorries became stuck, especially if the drivers were unfamiliar with the town and the narrowness of the passage.

Well do I remember the sight in 1952, when one particular lorry became stuck. Part of the vehicle was jammed fast, although the back wheels still protruded near the drinking fountain. Eventually after 3 days, the load was removed and the tyres let down, so that it could be dragged out slowly, without too much damage to the passage. The scrape marks were visible for several years afterwards.

The King's High School for Girls, Warwick. The Staff Room.

EASTGATE — THE MAIN SCHOOLROOM OVER THE ROADWAY. Once the main schoolroom used by the boys in the days of the Bablake School, the room was later adapted for use as a Living Room or Parlour. From 1918 it was used as a Staff Room by The King's High School For Girls and during the Second World War the Staff Fire-Watchers found the room a useful vantage point each night. After the war, the room was used as a classroom by Sixth Form Pupils.

Such happenings as that finally made the closure of the traffic arch a reality. In 1953, the Council decided to prohibit all traffic and there were various suggestions as to future improvements.

I was highly amused to read recently that in 1954, there had been a serious suggestion that a portcullis be placed either end of the arch. These were only to be raised on ceremonial occasions because various members of the Town Council were worried that "unauthorised and undesirable practices" would take place under the arch! I wonder what they were so worried about? Ornamental flower beds were tried for a time, but in the end, fortunately, the arch was left as it was.

A New Owner.

In 1983, the Trustees of King Henry VIII's Charity decided to sell what West's Directory of 1830 had called a "Beautiful little building." Expensive to maintain the building was felt to be a drain on the Charity purse. In due course, Mr John Adcock, a chartered accountant living in Lapworth, became the new owner. As his daughter had attended the King's High School, Mr Adcock knew the building well. The lease to King's High School still has several years to run and the public spirited gesture by John Adcock has been much appreciated. To own and safeguard such an important old building, so steeped in history, must give an enormous amount of pleasure.

Splendid Teachers!

It would seem that much of the success of the Girls' school was due to the excellent staff, many of whom stayed in their posts for a considerable number of years. Right from the start, the school was very fortunate in the selection of the teachers and loyalty and continuity became firmly established.

Over the years, there were so many teachers giving many years of service that I felt it would be inappropriate to single out specific names. As it is not the brief of this book to give a comprehensive history of the school, I thought it better to concentrate on the Head Teachers and let them represent all the other worthy women who served under them.

The Head Teachers.

1879 – 1895	Miss Fisher (Mrs Kelson)
1896 – 1913	Miss Lea (Mrs Gardner)
1913 – 1921	Miss Edgehill
1921 – 1922	Miss Gardner (Lady Moberly)
1922 – 1944	Miss Doorly
1945 – 1947	Miss Wiseman (Mrs Gunn)
1948 – 1970	Miss Hare
1970 – 1987	Miss Leahy
1987 –	Mrs Anderson

With Head Teachers and Deputy Heads providing stability at the top, strong bonds were formed within the school. From Headmistresses Miss Doorly, Miss Hare and Miss Leahy, together with their Deputies Miss Naish, Miss Whittlesey and Miss Greenwood, a staggering total of over 167 years of service was given.

Eleanor Doorly—A Famous Personality.

It would not be appropriate for me to describe in detail the lives of all the Headmistresses, who lived and worked in Landor House. I do not know much about many of them, except in their official capacity and most are now dead.

However one Headmistress was internationally famous, largely because she was a writer. From what I can discover, she had a vibrant personality, which impressed all those who came into contact with her. Some considered her eccentric, but that mattered little. Under her guidance the school blossomed into a fine institution and developed an excellent reputation, which has remained to this day.

So as I selected the Head Teachers to represent all the other staff who served under them, so I have chosen Eleanor Doorly as the representative of all the other Head Teachers.

The years from 1922 to 1944, when Miss Doorly was Headmistress, were also some of the most eventful years in English history. Miss Doorly's reign marked the transition from the old-fashioned way of life to modern times.

ELEANOR DOORLY

In January 1922, Victoria Eleanor Doorly was selected from 41 candidates to succeed Miss Gardner (Lady Moberly) as Headmistress and so began a marvellous period in the history of The King's High School For Girls. Under Miss Doorly's influence the school's reputation grew and many modern ideas concerning education were introduced. It is a tribute to the strong character of this woman that many residents of Warwick still remember her today, nearly fifty years after she left.

Born in 1880, of Irish descent, Eleanor Doorly was the daughter of Captain Anton Doorly. She was educated at Leamington High School and Ecole Normale, in Orleans, France. Later she went to London University and Cambridge Training College. In 1905, Miss Doorly obtained a B.A. (Honours) in Modern Languages (English and French) and in 1912, she obtained an M.A. Degree in History, also from London University. The title of her thesis "The Influence of English Diplomacy on Italy 1859 – 1861", perhaps explained her life-long love of that country. Since it has been suggested that she was born in Jamaica, it may well have been that members of her close family were Diplomats.

Her teaching career began in 1907 at Bradford Girls' Grammar School, but later that year she transferred to the North London Collegiate School, where she was an Assistant Mistress, specialising in History and English. She remained in that famous London School (where the pioneering Miss Buss had been Headmistress) for eight years, presumably studying for her History Degree in her spare time.

In 1915, she was appointed Headmistress of Twickenham County School and she remained in that post for seven years.

The Year 1922.

In many ways, 1922 was an interesting year. The first wireless broadcasts took place, 18 years old Johnny Weissmuller became the first man to swim the 100 metres in less than a minute, Tutankamen's tomb was discovered, Ghandi was sentenced to jail in India and The Irish Free State was set up. As regards women, Dr Ivy Williams was the first English woman to be called to The Bar and in Washington Mrs W. Felton was sworn in as the first woman senator in U.S.A.

England and the education of girls was in a state of transition. Only four years previously, at the end of the First World War, had women over 30 been given the vote and the younger women were to wait another six years before being enfranchised. Even though many women worked, few had the opportunity to take up a profession and generally women retired from work on marriage.

EASTGATE IN THE NINETEEN TWENTIES.
An unusually deserted Eastgate with the stonework near the section of town wall to the left, still looking fairly new. It would seem that this section of stonework was the remains of the extension to the Bablake School, which was demolished soon after 1875, when the Charity School closed. The Butts Entrance to the King's High School (door on left) was contructed in 1883. In this photograph, the old style telephone box and street gas lamp add atmosphere.

In Warwick, as elsewhere, small shops struggled to survive in the harsh, post-war period. A good Raleigh bicycle cost £10 and a dozen bottles of Amontillado sherry £3, but few could afford luxuries. Henry H. Lacy was the name above a prominent book and stationery shop in High Street and Landor House and the cottages were covered by a mass of creeper. The main Fire Station was situated in The Butts (between the traffic lights and the Tink-A-Tank) and the horse-drawn, steam driven, fire engine could often be heard, clattering past on its way to a fire.

Electric trams rattled past Landor House on their way to Leamington and my Great-Great Aunt, Mrs Selfe, kept a sweet shop and Refreshment Room in her tiny house in Smith Street, immediately opposite the cottages. Often visited by tram workers, who used to torment her parrot, Aunt Kate also served the boarders from Landor House and occasionally Miss Doorly herself.

In after years, when I visited the tiny shop, Aunt Kate always spoke very highly of Miss Doorly, whom she regarded as a wonderful personality and an asset to the town.

Headmistress of King's High School.

With two degrees and a wealth of teaching experience, the locally educated 42 year old woman must have seemed an ideal candidate for the post of Headmistress. With three Headmistresses in as many years, perhaps the Governors wanted an older woman who would be more likely to provide stability.

Within a year, new ideas were flooding through the school and, although some people were alarmed at first, the force of Eleanor Doorly's personality soon won over the critics.

At the root of her innovations was the idea that girls needed to become as well educated as possible, seeking more from life then merely becoming a wife. Miss Doorly reasoned that if more girls reached university standard, the universities would be forced to provide more places for girls, to satisfy the increased demand.

However, narrow minded "Blue Stockings" were not encouraged and home making was still considered important. If anything, she considered the less able girls needed more help and in 1929 she declared,

> "I hope you will see (a point about which I am very particular) that here every girl is of equal value and that the less brilliant have more, not less, of the school's attention."

Such worthy sentiments endeared her to many as did her attempts to offer the pupils many and varied experiences. Concerts and visits were arranged and a Music Club and School Orchestra flourished. The school was filled with good pictures; indeed it was said at one time that the King's High School had the best pictures of any school in England.

Although not beautiful, Eleanor Doorly was an attractive and commanding figure. Tall and rather thin, she had a prominent nose and large, expressive mouth. Her piercing eyes gave an air of confidence and her hair was usually drawn back in a loose bun. Yet according to all those who met her and judging from photographs, there was a certain sympathy which softened her features. Here was not a dragon of a headmistress, but an intelligent, capable, sincere personality, well able to understand the feelings of others.

Generally Miss Doorly wore dark coloured dresses or suits and was particular about her clothes. In later years, she carried a lorgnette and became slightly stooped, often with her head tilted a little to one side. However, the commanding presence of this magnetic personality was still apparent, even when she was well into her sixties.

It was not long before Miss Doorly had established a reputation for efficiency. As various innovations were introduced to broaden the outlook of pupils, it soon became clear that her approach was popular. The number of pupils rose from 361 to 523 within a few years and the 36 or so boarders seem to have been extremely happy on the whole.

Perhaps the secret of her success was that she was imaginative, but also believed in the old fashioned virtues. She impressed on the girls that personal honesty was

ELEANOR DOORLY.

A youthful portrait taken around 1910. The original of this photograph was given by Miss Doorly herself to Clara Wood — "My personal friend" as the grateful Headmistress used to refer to her general assistant, who did a variety of jobs, including looking after Vlah. After Clara left the school and married (married name Mrs Joynes) this photograph suitably framed in oak, had pride of place on the piano until Clara's death a couple of years ago.

LANDOR HALL IN THE NINETEEN TWENTIES.
Of all the rooms in Landor House, this room seems to have changed least. In the time of Miss Doorly, only the Boarders and Visitors would have seen much of this hall.

extremely important and that it was as bad to get off a bus without paying as it was to steal something from the counter in Woolworths'.

School and Form Councils.

The year after her arrival, Eleanor Doorly caused much controversy in some circles, by setting up a School Council to which every form in the school sent a representative. Each teacher and prefect also had a vote and although there were some motions which the Headmistress could veto, at least the pupils had some say in the running of their school. Later, a second member of each form was allowed to attend as an observer and this gave many pupils an insight into democracy.

The Form Representative was chosen in the Form Council, which took place weekly. These Form Councils were very useful for allowing the girls to discuss things which were bothering them, besides providing a practice ground for public speaking.

My cousin Betty Wright (née Blythe) who attended the school from 1936-41, recalled some amusing anecdotes concerned with the School Council. Each summer some form or other would propose that, "White ankle socks be allowed for tennis on the Playing Field."

Each summer, Miss Doorly would veto the proposal as improper. As the playing field of the Boys' School was on the other side of the hedge and illicit conversations were not uncommon, it was not considered desirable for the boys to glimpse the girls' knees! If the girls would promise to have knickers which always covered their knees, then socks would be appropriate, but if not, then the full-length, lisle stockings would continue to be worn for tennis.

The system of councils as instigated by Miss Doorly is still in use in the school, much as it was nearly 70 years ago. Even today, many Head Teachers would not be keen to give pupils such a platform from which to present any grievances. From 1923, thanks to Eleanor Doorly, the King's High School has led the way towards democratic government.

In an effort to bring about cooperation between parents and staff, again in 1923, Miss Doorly set up a Parents' Association. Although considered a daring, modern idea, this was generally welcomed after the initial shock had worn off.

Lectures.

To help the girls become better informed, "Aunt Do" as she was affectionately called, because she had said, "Think of me as an aunt," arranged many lectures by visiting speakers. She seemed to be friendly with many influential people and Walter De La Mare, John Galsworthy, Alfred Noyes, Laurence Housman, John Drinkwater, Sir Ronald Ross and many others came to speak. Recitals were arranged by such people as Jelly d'Aranyi, the famous violinist, and for many this was a first introduction to serious music, before gramophone records of such works became widely available.

Apparently every Wednesday morning Miss Doorly organised a lecture for the whole school. Sometimes there was a visiting speaker, but more often than not Miss Doorly gave the talk herself, perhaps explaining some aspect of current affairs, reading some poetry or merely giving the girls general advice.

This general advice often concerned cleanliness or gargling. Thorough daily washing and frequent baths were considered essential, as was gargling with water to which a few crystals of permanganate of potash had been added. Sometimes the virtues of deep breathing and exercise would be explained and the dire consequences in store for those who did not use their lungs properly were stressed!

Again Betty Wright had a marvellous story to relate concerning the morning lectures. Apparently some girl had lost a sum of money in school and Miss Doorly explained her lack of faith in the purses on strings, then in use for carrying money.

"It's far better to keep money in the pocket of your knickers," she theorised, pulling up her long navy skirt, to reveal navy knickers secured with elastic below the knee! Her purse was kept safe in a pocket, complete with flap and button, to prevent it falling out.

It may well have been that Miss Doorly liked to indulge in unexpected actions, just to make sure that the pupils never lost interest.

Awareness of Current Affairs.

Every effort was made to encourage the girls to be aware of current affairs. During the build up to the famous General Election of 1923, when Anthony Eden

VLAH IN A FAVOURITE POSITION.
Ears alert, listening for the slightest sound, Vlah loved to lie in front of the fire in Miss Doorly's
study.

(Conservative) beat Frances, Lady Warwick (amazingly standing for Labour) and others in the fight for the Warwick and Leamington seat, Miss Doorly and other teachers took parties of Sixth Formers to hear election addresses by the various candidates. Possibly having sympathy with the Socialist cause (many fair-minded intellectuals did in the harsh economic climate of the nineteen twenties) Miss Doorly took very seriously the task of educating girls to use their newly won voting rights. With no radio or television programmes to broadcast election information to the mass of the electorate, public meetings held great significance.

Wherever possible, parties of girls were taken on trips to broaden their knowledge. In 1927, Miss Doorly and another member of staff took a school party to Criccieth to watch the total eclipse of the sun. Even today such a trip would not be commonplace.

Vlah, the Faithful Alsation.

Over the centuries, Landor House seems to have attracted dog-lovers and Miss Doorly was no exception. Fond of animals in general, she had a large Alsation in her study, ready to growl or lick any visitors. The faithful Vlah (named after an Albanian word meaning friendship) was usually to be found on the mat in front of the fire or under the elegant roll-top desk. When Miss Doorly visited other buildings on the school site, Vlah's bark, as he escorted his mistress, often gave a warning signal of her approach.

Walks for Vlah were no problem as when the boarders went for their daily walk, the girl with no partner at the end of the crocodile, held Vlah on a lead. Those walks must have been one of the sights of Warwick at the time!

Vlah was a wonderful guard dog and anyone entering the study needed to beware. Some members of staff, being rather scared of him, hated to enter the room in Miss Doorly's absence, but sometimes Vlah took an instant liking to strangers. Miss G.M. Cadbury (who taught Botany and Biology) now 91 years young and still active, recalled recently that when she was interviewed for her first teaching post in 1926, Miss Doorly asked her to sit on the sofa and wait for a few minutes. As his owner finished her notes, Vlah walked quietly to Miss Cadbury and putting his paws on her shoulders, licked one side of her face with great enthusiasm. Poor Miss Cadbury, having taken great care with her appearance, wondered what her face might look like with one side powdered and the other well washed!

Perhaps all visitors were required to pass the Vlah Test? I have known many animal lovers who trusted the instinct of their dogs and who were very wary of those the animal disliked.

Mrs Betty Hawkins (née Wood)

A most interesting Warwick couple, Mrs Betty Hawkins and her husband Joseph, were able to supply much information concerning Miss Doorly. For many years Betty and sister Clara worked at the King's High School, carrying out a variety of tasks, including caring for Vlah during the school holidays, when his mistress was abroad. Miss Doorly treated Clara as a Personal Assistant and in gratitude, presented her with copies of her books personally signed. When Clara left the school to marry, she still kept in touch and visited Miss Doorly during her retirement.

Joseph amused me very much when he described how he and Miss Doorly had helped arrest a drunken Irish man outside Landor House in 1937. Betty and Joseph had been outside when the policeman was attacked by the man resisting arrest. Joseph was trying to restrain the struggling figure when Miss Doorly arrived on the scene with a rope to tie up his legs! She was not amused at the bad language and, following a Court appearance the next day, the unfortunate drinker was given an extra six months hard labour on his sentence for using insulting behaviour.

Animal lover Betty had obviously been devoted to Vlah and later she told of her sadness when she and Clara witnessed his accident as he slipped on a polished floor in Landor House and broke his hip. The Vet was unable to help the old dog and when Miss Doorly returned from holiday and went straight to the attic room, enquiring "Where's my Doggie?" thinking he was with the sisters, she learned the sad tidings from a tearful Clara.

"Miss Doorly took it very well," said Betty and the warmth of feeling towards her old employer was evident.

When Betty and Clara left the school, several years before her retirement, Miss Doorly was very sympathetic. "Never sacrifice the future for the past," she said and it was easy to understand why her former employees held her in such high regard.

A Famous Writer. Winner of Carnegie Medal in 1939.

Even without her other considerable accomplishments, Eleanor Doorly deserves to be remembered as an extremely famous writer of books for children. Although largely forgotten today, during the nineteen thirties and forties her books were best sellers and appeared in many editions and later as early Puffin paperbacks.

Her first book "England In Her Days Of Peace" published in 1920, whilst she was Headmistress of Twickenham County School, gave a fascinating social history of England. This book was later adopted as a text book by many Canadian schools, so her fame spread abroad.

Altogether she wrote 6 books, including "The Insect Man" (describing Henry Fabre) published in 1936, "The Microbe Man" (Louis Pasteur) in 1938, "The Story of France" in 1944 and "Ragmuffin King" (Henry IV of France) written in 1948, after she had retired.

"The Radium Woman" which told the story of Marie Curie, was published in 1939. This book won for Eleanor Doorly the famous Carnegie Medal and so her name is included in a select list of writers of books for children. Inaugurated in 1936 and named after the great Scottish born philanthropist Andrew Carnegie, who did so much to help public libraries, the Carnegie Medal is the most prestigious and eagerly sought award for children's literature. The medals, which have no cash value, are awarded by the Library Association, the professional body for librarians.

The first winner was Arthur Ransome for "Pigeon Post" to be followed by Eve Garnett for "The Family From One End Street" in 1937. Eleanor Doorly's triumph for the best children's book of 1939 was announced the following year when the news attracted little attention during the week following Dunkirk. The Warwick Advertiser of June 7th 1940 carried a tiny article, almost hidden away on page 3, which stated "Warwick Headmistress Honoured".

In after years, the list of winners included Eric Linklater, Walter De La Mare, Elizabeth Goudge, Mary Norton, Eleanor Farjeon, Rosemary Sutcliff, Penelope Lively and Richard Adams for "Watership Down". So the name of Eleanor Doorly is in the finest of company.

Friendship With Marjorie, Countess of Warwick.

Several people hinted that at times the intellectually brilliant Miss Doorly appeared rather a lonely person and this made her close friendship with Marjorie, Countess of Warwick all the more interesting.

The intelligent and capable Marjorie was a sister of the famous local M.P. Anthony Eden (afterwards Prime Minister from 1955-57 and later created Earl of Avon) and when her husband the 6th Earl died in 1928, she continued to live in the Castle until her eldest son became 21. From 1929 to 1931, she was Mayor of Warwick and at that time had many connections with the Governing Body of The King's High School.

Marjorie was a frequent visitor at Landor House during this period and Betty Hawkins gave amusing accounts of the elaborate cleaning operations which were carried out each time, prior to her arrival.

When she was young, Eleanor Doorly made a resolution never to visit any country whose language she could not speak and she became a brilliant linguist, fluent in several languages. Although not as academic as Miss Doorly, Marjorie too was an accomplished linguist; the two women sharing a passion for France. It would seem to be significant that during her time in Warwick Miss Doorly wrote five books about French people and France, two of them "The Insect Man" published in 1936 and "The Story of France" published in 1944, being dedicated to Marjorie.

By the time "The Story of France" appeared sadly Marjorie was already dead. She died in February 1943, aged only 56 and was laid to rest in the family vault in the crypt of St Mary's Church in Warwick. In 1944, Eleanor Doorly bought sixty flowering trees and shrubs which were planted outside the church in memory of Marjorie. Although most are now dead, a few still remain as a lasting reminder of their friendship. Marjorie's name is also perpetuated in the form of a prize, given appropriately for Oral French, which she endowed at The King's High School.

The Second World War.

Things must have been difficult for the aging Eleanor Doorly during the Second World War, but by all accounts she still maintained her liveliness and enthusiasm.

ELEANOR DOORLY, EDITH NAISH AND VLAH IN 1929.
This section of a photograph taken in 1929 shows Miss Doorly, a number of her senior staff and the faithful Vlah, who always seemed to be included on official photographs. From left to right, the back row is Miss Oldham (school secretary) Miss Cadbury, Miss Wheeler-Robinson, Miss Clark and Miss Gilbert. The middle row is Miss Sackett, Miss Naish, Miss Doorly and Mrs Coltart (Miss Powell). The front row is Helena Horler (prefect) Mary Bennett — Head Girl (Mrs Steele) and Helen Tyson (prefect).

Kings' High School for Girls, Warwick ∩ Dormitory.

LATER THIS COTTAGE ROOM BECAME MISS NAISH'S FORM ROOM.
In the Eighteenth Century, when these premises formed "The Coach and Horses Inn', no doubt many travellers stayed in this room. For much of the time after the premises became part of the King's High School, the room was used as a Dormitory for several girls. This photograph was taken in the 1920s and provides a fascinating glimpse of the simple accommodation offered. After 1945, when boarding ceased, Edith Naish used this room to tutor a Sixth Form Group and a large polished Victorian desk (probably one of the original purchases in 1879) became a much admired feature.

She tried to keep the girls informed about news items, sometimes even interrupting mealtimes to make announcements about the progress of the war.

Her linguistic skill and integrity enabled her to help the war effort by acting as a translator. For a number of years she had visited Norway annually and her fluent Norwegian and specialized knowledge were much in demand.

Like other buildings, Landor House had its windows protected by criss-crossed sticky tape, but as there was still old fashioned gas lighting, blacking out the lights at night did not present too much of a problem.

Four air-raid shelters were constructed; two being in the garden to the east of Red House Lawn, the other two being at the far end of the playground.

During the first year of the war, another school was sharing the buildings. King Edward VI Camp Hill School For Girls, Birmingham, was evacuated to Warwick and this must have caused Miss Doorly and Miss Naish many problems of organisation. The King's High School used the class rooms from 8 o'clock to 12 and Camp Hill from 2 o'clock till 6.

On 3rd and 4th June 1940, over 338,000 troops were rescued from the beaches at

*THIS DELIGHTFUL WALL WAS ONCE PART OF THE SMALLER COTTAGE —
NUMBER 3 SMITH STREET. Now a cloak-room, this first floor section leads to a Careers
Room, which can be glimpsed through the open door. Once Miss Naish's Form Room, it had
previously been a dormitory.*

Dunkirk and brought back to England in a variety of ships and small boats. This
legendary escape of the British Expeditionary Force even had repercussions in
Landor House. The hundreds of thousands of troops had to be accommodated
somewhere and barracks all over the country were overflowing as many train loads
of soldiers arrived in search of rest. Hundreds of men, displaced from the nearby
Budbrook Barracks sought hospitality in Warwick and many were forced to camp
out on the race-course for several days.

Betty and Joseph Hawkins described how Miss Doorly typically offered
hospitality to soldiers in need. They were invited into the garden and given
whatever food and drink was available.

I do not know how many soldiers were helped by Miss Doorly, but in the
"Warwick Advertiser" of June 7th 1940, there was a short article headed "A
Wonderful Manifestation" which described how serving men passing through the
town had benefited from the generosity and kindness of the people of Warwick.

Miss Doorly saw to it that everything possible was done to help the war effort. A
row of apple trees was planted in the garden, but the war was over by the time much
fruit was produced. However it seemed appropriate that fruit trees should have
been planted, more or less on the site once occupied by Ann Johnson's orchard.

ELEANOR DOORLY'S STUDY.
Still used as the Head Teacher's Study, this elegant room was once the Parlour in the time of the Johnsons. Much of the furniture and furnishings were Miss Doorly's own, but the table on the right would seem to figure in photographs of Landor Hall at other times.
In all probability, Eleanor Doorly wrote the first handwritten drafts of her most famous books sitting at her delightful roll-top desk to the right of the fire-place.

Like many other householders at the time, Eleanor Doorly kept chickens, so that eggs might supplement the meagre rations. Usually looking after the birds herself, she would often give a young visitor a freshly laid egg to take home for tea.

Edith Naish

I do not think one can give a comprehensive appreciation of the life and times of Eleanor Doorly, without mentioning Edith Naish. Inspirational as Miss Doorly was, she needed the help of an efficient Deputy Headmistress and this she found in Miss Naish.

She was appointed to the school in 1923, shortly after Miss Doorly herself. The two women worked side by side for the next 21 years, seeing the school through some difficult times, especially during the Second World War. Although Miss Doorly was praised for running the school very efficiently, I suspect much of the praise was due to the efforts of Edith Naish, working quietly in the background.

Possessing great organising ability, Miss Naish was a gifted Mathematics teacher, being able to communicate the most difficult of concepts to pupils who had little natural ability in the subject. It is said that she was ever present during the difficult war years and potential disasters were frequently overcome by sensible decisions. Both pupils and staff trusted her sense of justice and she was often asked to sort out disagreements. Always loyal to Miss Doorly and the school, she was an ideal working partner.

Although less in the limelight than Miss Doorly, Edith Naish was a great character in her own right. She retired in 1958 and the last time I ever saw her, she was explaining to a group of Old Girls how she had driven over 40 miles from her home in Wallingford, near Oxford, to visit her favourite dentist in Warwick. She was then in her mid eighties!

She died in July 1981, aged 89, in circumstances which many would consider appropriate. Having been her usual active self earlier on, she decided she was feeling very tired and declined to join her guest Miss Whittlesey in picking peas for dinner from the garden. So Miss Naish sat in her favourite chair for a little sleep and she never woke again.

Gladys Short (née Blakeman) Laboratory Assistant.

For 47 years, Gladys Short was the Laboratory Assistant and she had many stories to tell concerning Miss Doorly.

"A lady, that's the only word for her," proclaimed Gladys, when I chatted to her recently. Aged well over 80, Gladys' mind is as sharp as ever and I laughed heartily when she recounted the story of how she had been attacked by Miss Doorly's dog.

On the day before term started, Gladys had to walk through the room where Vlah was shut in. Although he knew her well, the dog was upset and tore her clothes so badly that she had to borrow some others from the much fatter cook. No blood was drawn, but Gladys had a nasty fright. Imagine her feelings next day when Miss Doorly sent for her and forced Vlah to shake hands!

"I was not at all keen to do so," admitted Gladys, "but I wouldn't make a fuss as the dog was usually well behaved and I thought so much of Miss Doorly".

It seemed that Miss Doorly always spoke to everyone in the same way, no matter what their status. Perhaps this was why she instilled such loyalty in all her staff, not only the teaching staff.

"I never heard anyone say a bad word about her, concluded Gladys and it was obvious from the way she spoke that there had been a mutual respect between the two women.

Retirement.

In 1944, the war news became more encouraging and it was obvious that great changes were imminent in Education, so at the end of the Autumn Term, at the age of 64, Eleanor Doorly retired from teaching.

She received many leaving presents including a cheque for £40 from the Old Girls and a gold watch and a cheque for £19 from the pupils of the school. Miss Naish, as

MISS DOORLY WITH VENN, IN RETIREMENT AT DARTMOUTH. 1946.

Second Mistress, presented a silver cigarette box, with a silver tea-service to follow, on behalf of "former and present members of staff." Typically Miss Doorly herself presented various things to the school, including five pictures from her own room.

One of her last official duties was to present the long serving Caretaker Mr Fallen with a gift of money for his invaluable service to the school. In her final assembly Eleanor Doorly's message to the whole school was that

> "You should have as your great aim in life the desire to make the world a happier place to live in."

Her short retirement was spent in Dartmouth, but she corresponded regularly with many of her old friends in Warwick. Some of them visited her at her home in High Town, where she enjoyed the companionship of another dog, Venn. She was always interested in the careers of her ex-pupils, especially some of the boarders, whom she had come to know particularly well.

She died in Dartmouth on 2nd May 1950, at the age of 70. Yet another victim of cancer, she was buried in Dartmouth.

Recently I have been privileged to examine the watch presented by the pupils of the school. Still in good working order, this handsome watch, with a broad band of old gold round the face, bore an inscription,

> "To Eleanor Doorly with love from the girls of K.H.S.W. Dec. 1944"

on the back. More than ever I wished I had known the recipient in the flesh.

I thought how fitting it was that after Miss Doorly's death this watch should have been left to Edith Naish. The two women had known each other for many years, since teaching together in London and in after years, Miss Naish always wore Miss Doorly's watch when attending the Old Girls' Dinner in Warwick, each Spring.

Still Remembered.

It is one of my great disappointments that I never met Eleanor Doorly. However, she appeared to have made a lasting impression on those who did know her and it says much for her character that generally she is remembered with great affection.

Many inhabitants of Warwick still remember her and only recently a woman was heard to remark, when girls from King's High School were blocking the pavement in The Butts, "They would never have behaved like that in Miss Doorly's day!"

I do not think this remark was intended as a slur against Head Teachers since 1944, or modern youth, but rather it was intended as a compliment to Miss Doorly's organisation. When she was appointed to Warwick, a Governor at her previous school spoke of her "practical Christianity" and perhaps this had much to do with her own high standards.

As I could never hope to capture all the essential qualities of such a complex and interesting woman, I thought it fitting that I allowed Eleanor Doorly herself, in the form of quotations from some of her letters, to have the last word.

The Letters of Eleanor Doorly.

Being a great communicator and multi-talented person, Eleanor Doorly wrote marvellous letters; the sort any recipient would treasure for years. Doubtless many friends and ex-pupils still preserve her letters, like an ex-boarder in Landor House, Pauline Molnar (née Curson).

Being one of the last boarders during the war, Mrs Molnar was still attending school when Miss Doorly retired in 1944, but there was an exchange of letters for the next five years. Via Mrs Molnar, Miss Doorly sent her love to the other boarders and signing herself "Yours affectionately," a warmth uncommon to retired teachers shone through.

The enquiring mind, the lively style and the balanced sentences of the accomplished writer are all evident in this selection of short quotations from the letters sent to Mrs Molnar. The earliest letter was written in 1945 and the last in May 1949, about a year before her death.

The last two letters were type-written and it was obvious that in 1948 Miss Doorly was suffering ill health for she wrote, "My thumb won't hold a pen and this machine tires the old lady."

However ill she may have been, her mind was still as alert as ever. If anything, the later letters are phrased more concisely and clearly.

Quotations From Eleanor Doorly's Letters.

Choice is a difficult matter. It is much easier and much duller to be set on a rail from which you can't escape.

Have you found the oxlips round Cambridge? They grow in quantity or used to. I have only found them on the road to Vezelay where Thomas of Canterbury made the speech that angered Henry II and very justly. I detest Thomas and therefore T.S. Eliot!

It is in the running for England's most beautiful village and certainly part of it might be useful to suggest housing in heaven. (Regarding the village of Dittisham in Devon.)

She was the dullest human being I remember. (When describing a brilliant woman scholar)

To make eggdusis—You throw an egg into a cup and heat it adding sugar, till the two are firm and frothy. Then you eat it with a spoon, cleaning the cup meticulously with a spoon and the spoon with your tongue.

THE REAR OF LANDOR HOUSE IN THE LATE NINETEEN SEVENTIES.
One of the few remaining patches of garden is almost lost under the snow. At one time, an
ancient vine and mulberry tree were to be found in this area.

I ask myself if I shall ever write a book again, but perhaps I shall have time when the garden is tidy and planted. ("Ragmuffin King" was published 3 year's later in 1948.)

How I sympathise about the burnt pans, drat them!

I think everyone should read "I Chose Freedom" to see how easily horror may descend on a country. It has turned me pale and set me writing to A.V. Alexander to beg him not to let the first anti-Magna Carta step come into the health bill. I daresay he thinks me a fool, but that a minister of state should have the right to dismiss without appeal to a common jury just horrifies me. I like a national health service. I have admired it in Norway and of course I see the minister's side, but not one single one of us should be punishable in the last resort except by the judgement of our peers. A.V. wrote me pages in reply, but I remain unconvinced. "Saints tumble to earth with so slight a tilt" In other words, it is so easy to slip down the incline into slavery. (Written in early 1948, before the introduction of the National Health Service)

Can the learned people with whom you consort tell me anything of the origin of Grammar? I find it most strange that the more primitive the language, the more grammar it has. How therefore did grammar begin?

I have been reading all De La Mare over again and find that no ugly word or thought has ever blotted his page. I know him well also and have never found a blot on his life.

Live your own life and when you find the man whose life you want to live, happy you. A married woman has to live her husband's life. I see no way out.

I love Chaucer, man and work. I am glad you do.

A profession must be hard to choose in these days, with all paths open to women.

I think one is almost safe in saying no time has been as difficult and therefore as interesting as this.

So many pleasures have come to me through seeing the other fellow's view.

So few people know what a great race the Arabs once were. How all the things we care for most they gave to Spain between the 8th and 15th centuries and how, as usual, the persecutor destroyed his own country in getting rid of the persecuted.

People like you to enjoy yourself. It's the grumbler who gets no invitations.

I have a perpetual invitation to my much loved Rome, but I can't imagine getting there again, alas!

(Regarding a close early friend) She wanted me to marry, but understood that when one has met the only man and he impossible to marry one must remain single.

I am quite sure that life is a matter for rejoicing, even viewed from the angle of permanent ill-health. I would not mind mine all over again and it has not been an easy one. (Written two years before her death)

SOME LAST SOBERING THOUGHTS

Few people realise that in 1947, there were drastic proposals for the town of Warwick, not least for Landor House and the area around Eastgate.

In a book entitled "Warwick. Its Preservation and Redevelopment"—a plan for the Borough of Warwick by P. Abercrombie and R. Nickson, startling proposals were outlined. There was to be a pedestrian concourse in front of Landor House, which was to become a Community Centre. The King's High School For Girls was to be moved elsewhere. The lower end of Chapel Street was to be diverted and the lower end of The Butts widened. A new road was then to be made across what is now the school playground to link The Butts, Chapel Street and a proposed new shopping centre.

Fortunately, these plans did not come about and Landor House and the rest of the property was left in much the same state as it had been for decades. Had the school moved, I might never have experienced the delights of the buildings and this book would not have been written.

However old or interesting they are, buildings need to be used to be certain of a bright future. A few months ago, in a National Daily newspaper, an Architect wrote a sensible letter describing how buildings needed to be used in order to survive. If the fabric of the building was respected and repairs carried out in like materials, the property could be made to last for many centuries. Only when buildings were extensively altered and made to fulfil purposes for which they were never intended was deterioration hastened.

So far, Eastgate, Landor House and the cottages seem to have survived remarkably well. With all the buildings being in the care of Charity Trustees since 1733, repairs have been carried out when necessary, but expensive alterations have been few. Admittedly the cottages were much altered when they were incorporated into the school in the latter years of the last century, but many features such as original beams, floors and cupboards remain. Eastgate is remarkably little altered and seems to possess a wonderful atmosphere, nurtured over the centuries by thousands of children as they laughed or cried over their schoolwork! As to Landor House, although some of the rooms, especially those in the Chapel Street wing, are substantially changed, basically the house is still that described in such detail by James Fish in 1733. The windows may be the wrong type, but they have been there for so long, that they too have become part of the history.

The study of history often seems to answer many questions which occur in our own times. Somehow it is comforting to realise that over the centuries the basic

DRY ROT CAN CAUSE HAVOC IN OLD BUILDINGS. During the nineteen seventies, dry rot was discovered in the large first floor room in Landor House. Now used as a Staff Room, it was once a large classroom. The main staircase can be seen through the open door.

needs and emotions of people have changed very little. Clothes and machines may be different, but parents still grieve for their children and house-owners still have arguments with their neighbours over boundary hedges. There are plenty of children around today who might be termed "lazy, undutiful and wild" exactly as Henry Johnson was in 1694 and the way in which the rebellious Walter Savage Landor spoke to his parents sounded very familiar! In general, the more I study old buildings, the more I am aware of the frailty of the human race.

An interesting reminder of the complex history of this site was provided in October 1960. During excavations in connection with the building of two classrooms in Landor House garden, to the rear of Red House lawn, a fairly complete skull was found. The site had been occupied by an air-raid shelter during the Second World War, so the depth of 5 feet at which the skull was found was more likely to have been 8 feet or more below normal ground level.

After investigation by experts at the Anatomy Department of Birmingham University, the skull was pronounced to be that of a man, aged between 35 and 45,

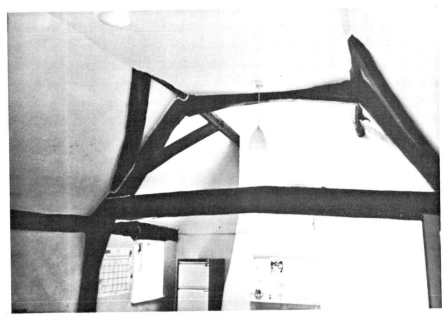

THESE MAGNIFICENT BEAMS, RECENTLY UNCOVERED, ARE IN AN UPPER ROOM OF THE LARGER COTTAGE. Once housing the Cottage Library, the room is now a Careers Room.

who probably lived in Medieval times. The teeth were good, apart from a large carious cavity in an upper right molar, which probably caused much toothache.

To anyone with a lively imagination, this discovery was fascinating. Where was the rest of the skeleton? Despite investigation in 1960, only a few animal bones (part of the right femur of a sheep and three long fragments of bovine bones) had been found nearby. Was the skull from a severed head once exhibited on Eastgate or had the skull once possessed by Dr Johnson been buried in the garden? It seems more than likely that the site in question was once occupied by the town ditch, so all manner of rubbish may have been dumped there afterwards.

What of the future? Doubtless the present pupils of the school, now in the care of Mrs Anderson and her Governors, will stamp their own identity on the site, but I hope things will not change too much. Always an optimist, I like to think of Ann Johnson's gift being appreciated in hundreds of years' time and Eastgate, which has stood for 500 years and more, standing for another 500 years!

I'll admit to being biased as my ancestors have lived in or near the town for hundreds of years, but most agree that Warwick is a most interesting and beautiful town. Much is known about its history, but much still remains to be discovered. I have gained enormous pleasure from studying this site—I hope that in the future others will find out even more of the fascinating history of this wonderful group of buildings.

CONTRASTS IN ARCHITECTURE.
Close inspection of the roof and projecting wings of Landor House illustrate how the previous dwellings occupying the site were adapted into the town house. The front door of Landor House continued the line of the Tudor cottages.

APPENDIX
LANDOR HOUSE 1692 – 1992

PROMINENT INHABITANTS AND FREQUENT VISITORS

1)   Dr William Johnson. Original owner. 1643 – 1725
2)   Ann Johnson—wife of William. Began Charity. 1648 – 1733
3)   James Fish the Younger—Famous surveyor. 1673 – 1740 *Vis.*
4)   Francis Smith—architect and builder. 1672 – 1738 *Vis.*
5)   Thomas Archer M.P. Later Baron of Umberslade. 1695 – 1768
6)   Dr Walter Landor—father of poet. 1733 – 1805
7)   Elizabeth Savage—heiress. Mother of poet. 1743 – 1829
8)   Maria Arden—heiress. 1764 – 1808
9)   Walter Savage Landor—World famous poet. 1775 – 1864
10) Henry Eyres Landor—land agent. Brother of poet. 1780 – 1866
11) Robert Eyres Landor—writer. Brother of poet. 1781 – 1869
12) Dr William Lambe—Analysed Spa Water. Vegetarian. 1765 – 1847 *Vis.*
13) Samuel Parr—Scholar. Adviser of Whig Politicians. 1747 – 1825 *Vis.*
14) R.C. Heath—Clerk to King's Schools Governors. 1833 – 1913 *Vis.*
15) Eleanor Doorly—Headmistress K.H.S. Famous writer. 1880 – 1950
16) Marjorie, Countess of Warwick. 1887 – 1943 *Vis.*
     Vis—Frequent visitor.